SO-AMK-464

Adult Literacy & American Identity

Adult Literacy
& AMERICAN IDENTITY

The Moonlight Schools &
Americanization Programs

SAMANTHA NECAMP

Southern Illinois University Press
Carbondale

Copyright © 2014 by the Board of Trustees,
Southern Illinois University
All rights reserved
Printed in the United States of America

17 16 15 14   4 3 2 1

Cover illustration: class of Mexican mothers in California
learning to read and write. From Cora Wilson Stewart,
Moonlight Schools for the Emancipation of Adult Illiterates (1922)

Library of Congress Cataloging-in-Publication Data
NeCamp, Samantha.
Adult literacy and American identity : the Moonlight schools
and Americanization programs / Samantha NeCamp.
   pages cm
Includes bibliographical references and index.
ISBN 978-0-8093-3358-5 (paperback)
ISBN 0-8093-3358-9 (paperback)
ISBN 978-0-8093-3359-2 (ebook)
1. Literacy—Appalachian Region—History—20th century.
2. Adult education—Appalachian Region—History—20th
century. 3. Americanization. I. Title.
LC5147.A67N43 2014
374'.0124—dc23   2014009017

Printed on recycled paper. ♻

The paper used in this publication meets the minimum
requirements of American National Standard for
Information Sciences—Permanence of Paper for
Printed Library Materials, ANSI Z39.48-1992. ∞

CONTENTS

ACKNOWLEDGMENTS

First and foremost, I thank Carol Mattingly, Lisa Arnold, and Vanessa Kraemer Sohan for reading more versions of this text than I'm sure any of us care to remember. Their feedback was essential, and this book would not exist without them. Thanks also to Kristine Priddy for her belief in this work and her patience during the editing process. In addition, Karen Kopelson, Bronwyn Williams, Connie Kendall Theado, Susan Ryan, Alicia Brazeau, and two anonymous reviewers provided much-appreciated advice and helpful commentary on earlier versions of this book. Thanks to my parents, Denise and John Vibbert, and mother- and father-in-law, Judy and John NeCamp, for logistical support as I researched and composed this text. My husband, John, and my son Desmond deserve special thanks for their support and patience, and my newest additions, Jackson, Isaac, and Eleanor, deserve thanks for being the motivation to finally put the finishing touches on this work. To all of you, my deepest appreciation.

Adult Literacy & American Identity

1. INTRODUCTION

*T*his book traces two rhetorics of literacy crisis—the immigrant and Appalachian literacy crises that became the focus of public discourse between 1910 and 1935—considering in particular the very different educational enterprises each sparked. Both the Americanization movement and the Moonlight Schools sought to provide literacy instruction to adults marked as illiterate. In doing so, the groups initiated a public discourse surrounding literacy that continues to shape perceptions of what it means to be literate and to teach literacy in the United States.

Immigrants and Illiteracy

Between 1890 and 1910, thirteen million immigrants arrived in the United States (Carlson 80), many of whom were southern and eastern Europeans. While previous large influxes of immigrants, such as those of Irish and northern European settlers in the 1840s and 1850s, had spawned violent reactions from "native" US residents, these reactions were most often framed in terms of race and ethnicity, the latter of which was perceived to include religious identity; that is, immigrants' "difference" was perceived as an innate quality that was difficult if not impossible to alter (see Ignatiev; Horsman). The "new" immigrants arriving at the turn of the century likewise inspired xenophobia, but unlike previous anti-immigrant reactions, the key "differences" identified between immigrants and natives were not (only) racial and ethnic but linguistic and educational. Indeed, as Connie Kendall has argued, the 1911 publication of the *Dictionary of Races or People* by the Dillingham Commission on immigration introduced a sweeping change in how the federal government—and, by extension, the general public—imagined and quantified race. Whereas immigrants' race had previously been "determined" by their country of origin, the Dillingham Commission's *Dictionary* led to a new form of classification: race was determined by one's language rather than one's nativity. Fears about immigrants' difference were thus written onto language and language performance. As such, literacy became a key marker of assimilation, worthiness, and American identity, because literacy "stood in" for racial and social difference.

Particularly following the 1900 and 1910 censuses, the perception that immigrants were illiterate spawned a rhetoric of literacy crisis that identified the illiteracy of immigrants as a threat to society as a whole. As one commentator argued in 1915, "illiteracy is a barrier to democracy," and "the first requisite for a government by representation is literacy" (Talbot 873). This illiteracy, he asserted, occurred mostly "among herded aliens, mingling foreign tongues in village outskirts and city slums, increasing accident and disease, filling hospitals, almshouses and asylums, and, as dependents and defectives, laying big and yet bigger taxes on that community which ignores their existence" (Talbot 875). Similarly, educator Ella Thorngate lamented in 1920 that the "thousands [of immigrants] who live together in 'colonies' in the congested sections of great cities, still holding to the language, customs, and manners they brought with them" called into question the "melting pot" model of American identity (123). Moreover, illiterate immigrants degraded native educational opportunities; the Board of Associated Charities, for instance, argued that "the difficulty of securing universal education is greatly increased when every year sees landed an army of one hundred thousand illiterates, whose children will start upon their career as American citizens from ignorant homes, under practically foreign surroundings" (qtd. in Ward 229).

For Thorngate, Winthrop Talbot, and many other commentators, illiteracy and a lack of English fluency marked immigrants as different and as threats to democracy both directly, through their inability to participate in public debate, and indirectly, through the strain immigrants placed on existing social structures. The rhetoric employed by both Talbot and the American Board of Charities implies that immigrants' educational needs would stretch the existing educational system to a point at which few students would receive an adequate education. Reflecting the perceived connection between illiteracy and un-American identity, nearly every legislative session between 1891 and 1917 voted on bills that sought to impose immigration restrictions through the use of a literacy test (see Hall),[1] emphasizing that the primary difference between "desirable" and "undesirable" Americans was literacy ability.

Because the threat posed by new immigrants was imagined in linguistic terms, the threat did have a remedy. While racial and ethnic identity could not be changed, language could be taught. By educating immigrants in English and in literacy skills, natives could defuse the threat posed by immigrant illiteracy, creating a literate public that could support democratic government and preserve "traditional" American values. More important, the process of educating immigrants reified the narrative of America as a land of opportunity and the appropriateness of middle class values by "symbolically assign[ing] status to those adhering most closely to the culture of native-born Americans" (Olneck 416). As Michael R. Olneck suggests, the act of teaching immigrants "also assigned to native-born Americans the roles of tutor, interpreter, and gatekeeper, while rendering immigrants the subjects of tutelage and judgment. Doing Americanization symbolically constructed or enacted a relationship of benevolent control and social superiority between native and newcomer" (416). By enacting control through an educative relationship (rather than the overt legislation or discrimination that had most frequently characterized earlier anti-immigrant sentiment), the literacy crisis surrounding "new" immigrants reestablished the public narrative of meritocratic success: if immigrants failed to succeed, it would be because of personal or moral failings, not because of lack of opportunity. This rhetoric served to reinforce existing class relationships by attributing class position to individual effort and achievement rather than social structures.

The rhetoric of literacy crisis that marked immigrants as different and threatening, and by extension, as in need of instruction, relied on a particular public image of what it meant to be "American": to be American, crisis rhetoric insisted, was to be literate and to participate in civic life. But the rhetoric of literacy crisis itself came under threat following each census cycle from 1880 to 1910, each of which reveals that the majority of illiterate people in the United States were native-born whites rather than immigrants.[2] Because native-born whites were imagined as the ideal of US citizenry, the "revelation" that many native people were, in fact, illiterate presented a rhetorical challenge to those who sought to impose American values on immigrants through education. To promulgate the image of the immigrant as a threat to civic life, crisis rhetoric had to emphasize the link between literacy and American identity and to depict immigrants as less literate than the general public. But for this equation to work, crisis rhetoric had to explain the existence of a large number of illiterate native-born whites, particularly those illiterate native-born whites—Appalachians—who had long been imagined as prototypical Americans. More important, the existence of illiterate Appalachians had to be excused and eliminated in such a way as to preserve Appalachians' status as exemplary Americans.

Early Appalachia: A Historical, Theoretical Site of Literacy Crisis

Lee Soltow and Edward Stevens's *The Rise of Literacy and the Common School in the United States*, published in 1981, is among the first major, comprehensive examinations of the history of US literacy. As such, it is a formative text for the field of literacy studies, a text that can be read as creating as issues the topics that are now the common ground of literacy studies. In their study, Soltow and Stevens employ Appalachia as a limit case through which to test and illustrate the effects of social, educational, and economic structures on literacy attainment. The region, they argue, "represents the extremes of illiteracy, an absence of centralized authority, and a lack of social concentration" (23) and is an example of "a vicious cycle of illiteracy, immobility, and lack of economic opportunity" (185). The authors point out that in the 1840 census, four of the ten counties nationally "with the highest illiteracy rates were located in this region" and that "one of these counties, Pike County, was the land of the feuding Hatfields and McCoys. Another was 'Bloody Breathitt,' which had earned an international reputation for its murderous activity" (185).

Because of their influential role within the discipline of literacy studies, Soltow and Stevens have, in effect, created a theoretical literacy crisis. Their use of Appalachia as a test case for the development of literacy—a test case chosen because the usual accoutrements of culture are, they suggest, absent from the region—depicts the area and its people as outliers in an increasingly literate public. They suggest that nineteenth-century Appalachia, more than any other region in the United States, should be taken as the archetype of an illiterate society. In its "extremes," its "vicious[ness]," its "lack," Appalachia is beyond the pale of normal developments in the history of literacy. It is, in effect, the "other" against which Soltow and Stevens create their "norm." In fact, we can only understand what it has meant to be literate in American history through the lens of the intergenerational, exceptionally high illiteracy of nineteenth-century Appalachia.

I highlight Soltow and Stevens's discussion of Appalachia not to cast aspersions on their thorough and detailed work but because Soltow and Stevens's rhetorical creation of an Appalachian literacy crisis within the context of literacy studies mimics, on a small scale, the larger cultural "invention" of Appalachia as "a strange land and peculiar people" (Batteau 15) characterized by "stereotypical feuds, moonshine stills, mine wars, environmental destruction, joblessness, and human depredation" (Eller ix). In particular, Soltow and Stevens's use of Harry Caudill's *Night Comes to the Cumberlands* to document not only historical immigration to the region but also the "story" of its inhabitants as "one which saw cynical, angry, and penniless outcasts come to America as indentured servants and finally escape to freedom in Eastern Kentucky" (185) is a reflection of the "myth of Appalachia" and its continuing power (Shapiro). Present-day impressions of Appalachians as violent and poor create a historical Appalachia of angry, penniless outcasts—despite the fact that Caudill cites no primary sources to document the attitudes and personalities of early settlers.

It is not surprising that Soltow and Stevens rely on Caudill's book to characterize Appalachians. As Allen Batteau explains, *Night Comes to the Cumberlands* is "more than any other single book or article . . . responsible for the resonant image of Appalachia held by the American public" (4–5). Yet, scholars have documented Caudill's "slipshod and poorly documented research, striking inconsistencies in his thought, his genetic theory of Appalachian development, his cultural elitism, [and] his failure to acknowledge the extent of citizen resistance in the mountains" (Fisher 284), as well as Caudill's inaccurate portrayal of mountain people as "unsophisticated and childish, easy game for clever lawyers and land speculators" (Eller 24).

Despite their problematic reference to Caudill, Soltow and Stevens's central evidence is (relatively) incontrovertible: Appalachians did record higher rates of illiteracy than the general public in census reports throughout the nineteenth century. Though illiteracy rates produced by the census cannot be read as numerically accurate—because enumerators relied solely on direct response to the questions "Can you read?" and "Can you write?" with no standardized measuring tool to assess respondents' abilities—many scholars, including Soltow and Stevens, employ census data to determine relative rates of literacy. While some census respondents may have under- or overrepresented their literacy, this "error" would remain constant across regions (and, for that matter, within age, sex, or race categories). Hence, census "figures lend themselves to interregional and intergroup comparisons as well as comparisons over time" (Soltow and Stevens 6). Similarly, education in Appalachia certainly lagged far behind other regions. Poverty and feuds *were* part of the social fabric of Appalachian life in both the nineteenth and early twentieth centuries (though, as many scholars have demonstrated, neither was as prevalent as the dominant images of Appalachia would suggest [see, for example, Billings, Norman, and Ledford]).

But as Batteau has argued, attempting to understand or undo the myth of Appalachia by appealing to historical realities misses the point: the cultural value of the "mountaineer" image is not and has never been tied to the accuracy of that image but to "the poetic values of the image" (6). He cautions, "This is why Caudill and his epigoni will continue to be read, while their critics, attacking a poetic text on ground of semantic inaccuracy, will not" (6). The "invention" of Appalachia, like the invention of all myths, had less to do with any attempt to accurately depict Appalachian life and more to do with the needs of those who hold power—in this case, "urban elites" (Batteau 1) and Americanization advocates who sought to differentiate immigrants from native-born Americans.

It is not coincidental, Batteau suggests, that the image of Appalachia as a land of "freedom-loving, wild, and lawless people" was "elaborated at the very same time that the relationships of external domination and control of the Southern Mountain Region's natural and human resources were being elaborated" (15). This elaboration was not based on new information about the region—as Soltow and Stevens suggest, evidence of Appalachian poverty and illiteracy was (re)produced and publicized with each new census—but rather "followed from the recognition that the well-known realities of southern mountain life were not consonant with new notions about the nature of America and American civilization which gained currency during this period [around 1870]. . . . [W]hat had seemed normal or at least explicable came after 1870 to seem nonnormal and inexplicable" (Shapiro xi). I argue that these "new notions about the nature of America and American civilization" were elaborated in response to the beginnings of "new" immigration, in response to the need for a narrative that differentiated immigrants from native-born citizenry.

This understanding of Appalachia as the "other" of America created a rationale for intervention. Coal and timber companies could frame their takeover of Appalachia as a civilizing effort: where previously there had been no economy, coal companies created one; where previously there had been no infrastructure, coal companies created it. Similarly, home missionaries "imposed a . . . vision of Appalachia as an area in need of assistance from outside agencies" (Shapiro xiii)—in need not because of the "particular conditions which prevailed in the southern mountains, of which they knew very little" but because of "the anomaly of Appalachia's existence as a discrete region of the nation" (xv). Missionaries and the philanthropists who supported their work sought to offer religion and education to "needy" Appalachians, resulting in a spread of dual purpose church missions/schools throughout the region (xiii, 62).

To find monetary and moral support for their work, these missionary educators employed a rhetoric of crisis. William Goodell Frost, president of Berea College from 1892 to 1920, is credited by many Appalachian scholars as the primary inventor of the image of Appalachia that dominated the early twentieth century (see Batteau; Shapiro). Frost taps into nascent nativist reaction to the wave of "new" immigrants in order to suggest that Appalachians were the last bastion of an uncorrupted Anglo-Saxon heritage—but a bastion under threat both from external forces and from its own poor educational system. Frost explains, "The ancestry of the mountain folk is for the most part creditable. . . . [I]t is almost wholly Revolutionary and British" (5). Furthermore, "as Appalachian America has received no foreign immigration, it now contains a larger proportion of the 'Sons' and 'Daughters' of the Revolution than any other part of the country" (3), and its people possess the "characteristics [that] are the exact complement of those which we now consider American" (8). By linking Appalachians to American identity, Frost posits the threats facing Appalachia as threats to the very idea of America. Calling for increased efforts (and money) toward educating Appalachians, he argues that "the question is whether the mountain people can be enlightened and guided so that they can have a part in the development of their own country, or whether they must give place to foreigners and melt away like so many Indians" (9). Frost also suggests that foreigners may have a corrupting influence on Appalachians if activists do not step in to educate the mountaineers: "[I]t is pitiful to see how helpless these people are in estimating the things of the outside world. 'Furriners' have impressed them with the wonders of train and telegraph, and they have no standard from which to decide where credulity should stop" (8).

Framed in these terms, Appalachian ignorance and backwardness were crises of American national identity. Appalachians posed a threat to the future of American identity in two ways. Concretely, their ignorance, as Frost suggests, creates a risk that they will be swayed by "foreign" influences, thus doubling the danger of immigrants' incursion into American life. If Appalachians were the embodiment of American history and character, their heritage and culture had to be preserved. But this preservation could only happen through education: until Appalachians were "graded up" to meet the standards of flatland society, their culture remained under threat both from industry and, more important, from the immigrants who were increasingly filtering in to the region to work in those industries. When the 1910 census reilluminated high levels of illiteracy throughout the country, the literacy crisis reached a fever pitch: although immigrants received much of the blame for the startling statistics, the crisis rhetoric employed to fund Appalachian settlement schools and reform efforts also flourished.

Less explicitly but no less clearly, Appalachians posed a threat to the narrative of immigrant difference. If immigrants were to be educated into assimilation on the grounds that their illiteracy marked them as different, the existence of a massive population of illiterate Appalachians threatened this narrative: while Appalachians existed (or at least while they existed in the larger American consciousness), the narrative of American meritocracy and the need for immigrant education could not be adequately sustained. Not only did the idea of Appalachian illiteracy construct Appalachians as an "other" to literate America but Appalachia's status as a preserve of American values turned its illiteracy rates from a reflection of the region's peculiarity into an issue of cultural and racial defense.

Crises in Parallel

Neither the Appalachian literary crisis nor the immigrant literacy crisis that peaked in the second decade of the twentieth century can be said to have "ended": literacy crises never "end"; they merely fade into the background of public discourse. Both scholars and the popular press continue to frame Appalachian illiteracy as both exceptional in nature and as a symbol of the region's depredation. For instance, Edward Gordon and Elaine Gordon write, "As many as 44 percent of Kentucky residents are functionally illiterate, according to a 1996 survey by the University of Kentucky" (296); a *20/20* television special in 2007, "A Hidden America: Children of the Mountains," includes illiteracy alongside incest, prescription-drug abuse, and toothlessness as both symptoms and causes of the region's extraordinary poverty. Similarly, immigrants continue to be the subject of much vitriolic rhetoric that posits their inability to speak English—and, by extension, their "illiteracy"—as a threat to American identity; as Bruce Horner and John Trimbur point out, advertisements published during the 1999–2000 Iowa caucuses "blamed immigrants for suburban sprawl, environmental degradation, and the corruption of politics" (609) and declared, "[S]ome [immigrants] don't even care about our heritage. So, they don't speak our language, and they create their own countries within ours. . . . take jobs and social services from our poorest citizens. . . . Expand our welfare rolls. And divide our nation" (American Immigrant Control Foundation qtd. in Horner and Trimbur 609).

Nor are these crises unique. In addition to the historical crises explored here, Appalachia and immigrants have been the subjects of multiple rhetorical moments of "crisis." Though the rhetoric of immigrant literacy crisis waned in the 1930s thanks to the advent of the Great Depression and restrictive immigration policies, a new crisis arose both during World War II—most painfully represented in the internment of Japanese Americans—and immediately afterward, when postwar prosperity once again made the United States an attractive destination for economic (and religious, social, and political) refugees. The rhetoric of Appalachian literacy crisis similarly peaks and wanes, with perhaps the most attention devoted to literacy issues in the wake of President Lyndon Baines Johnson declaring his War on Poverty while standing on a ramshackle front porch in eastern Kentucky in 1964.

In spite of the continuous pattern of peaks and troughs in the rhetoric of literacy crisis, the particular moments of crisis highlighted in the current volume share many features. In particular, the two intertwined crises inspired educational interventions that redefined both "literacy" and the idea of literacy education. In 1911, in response to the rhetoric of Appalachian literacy crisis, educators in Rowan County, Kentucky, formed the Moonlight Schools movement, a movement some historians have termed "the official beginning of literacy education in the United States" (Cook 13). Though the Moonlight Schools were not the beginning of literacy education, they were the first program to suggest that all adults—and especially illiterate adults—should be given the opportunity to attend schools and that these schools should employ pedagogies and methods specifically designed to address adult student populations. Founded by Cora Wilson Stewart, a native eastern Kentuckian working as a schoolteacher and superintendent, the pedagogies the Moonlight Schools employed drew from local experience (and, in so doing, granted legitimacy to those experiences) and granted students some hand in determining curriculum. The immigrant literacy crisis inspired the creation of "Americanization" programs that sought to instruct immigrants in the English language and aspects of American culture (including government and history but also food preparation, child care, and hygiene). A wide variety of groups developed Americanization programs, including businesses, women's clubs, and charitable organizations. Though they were not developed as a comprehensive, centralized educational system, as were the Moonlight Schools, most groups shared similar pedagogies and public appeals, and Americanizers of all stripes slowly coalesced through the development of conferences and professional organizations to support Americanization educators.

Extra-Institutional Literacy Education

About their rationale for composing a history of education, H. Warren Button and Eugene F. Provenzo Jr. explain: "Teachers and other professional educators need to know the histories of the institutions that educate and of their roles within them. Without knowledge of their pasts, of how they have come to be and how they have changed or have failed to change, these institutions and roles cannot be understood and, therefore, cannot be intelligently improved" (1). I argue that a more complete understanding of the Moonlight Schools and Americanization programs can help literacy educators understand how the study of literacy has come to be, has changed, and has failed to change. As Jacqueline Jones Royster explains, "[W]e gain in an understanding of literacy in general from views of literacy in its particulars, from placing the 'thick description' of the literate practices of a particular group in the company of similar descriptions of other groups" (6). Here, I place the literacy education practices of two groups in dialogue with one another, two groups that can also speak to larger developments within the history of literacy and its teaching. The two movements represent a shift in the history of literacy because they fostered a public discourse concerned not only with illiteracy but also specifically with literacy education. Furthermore, the two groups engaged the general public in the act of literacy teaching to a degree not seen before or since. I argue in particular that the public perceptions of teaching writing fostered by the public debate between the Moonlight Schools and Americanization played a key role in the professionalization (or lack thereof) of literacy educators.

In its public battles with Americanization advocates, the Moonlight Schools movement created a public discourse about what it means to be literate and what it means to "teach writing" that set the terms for later crises and responses. The Moonlight Schools were well covered in national newspapers, beginning as early as 1912 with a feature article in the *Washington Post*. Perhaps more important, Moonlight Schools advocates and Americanizers came to dominate educational discourse by presenting at the National Education Association's national convention and by staging their own conferences. In particular, the Moonlight Schools' push for volunteer teaching and the Americanizers' demand for trained teachers created a paradoxical public rhetoric of writing instruction, a rhetoric that both insisted that "anyone" could teach writing and simultaneously blamed teachers (and their lack of training) for high illiteracy rates. This paradoxical attitude toward literacy instruction recurred throughout the twentieth century and continues into the twenty-first: in the scathing attitude toward schooling seen in the 1950s literacy crisis the publication of *Why Can't Johnny Read* provoked; in the

1970s college-based literacy crisis Merrill Sheils's essay "Why Johnny Can't Write" inspired; and most recently, in the teacher-and-school-punishing system of testing the No Child Left Behind Act of 2001 developed. I contend that the history of the Moonlight Schools and Americanization programs can shed light on the development of attitudes toward literacy education and educators that might better position current literacy educators to respond to ongoing discourses of literacy crisis.

Two Responses to Rhetorics of Literacy Crisis

The Appalachian and immigrant rhetorics of literacy crises each sparked an educative program designed to remedy the "problems" illiterates posed. In Appalachia, the Moonlight Schools offered evening classes to adults. Courses, held in local school buildings, were taught by volunteer teachers, usually day-school educators who were from the local area. The program focused on basic literacy and numeracy. Moonlight Schools supporters claimed that the pedagogy developed for the schools could teach literacy in as little as six weeks, in part because the courses were taught and organized by local educators and the materials based on local sources, inspiring both trust and interest among students. Based on a wildly successful initial program in eastern Kentucky, the schools became a nationwide program, and founder Stewart became the most recognized authority on literacy issues in the 1920s. Her success culminated in her appointment as chairperson of the first governmental organization that targeted illiteracy: the National Advisory Committee on Illiteracy.

Her chairpersonship put Stewart in direct conflict with immigrant education specialists. While immigrant education programs had existed throughout US history, the influx of new immigrants inspired widespread devotion to the cause of immigrant education, particularly among industries and clubwomen. These groups, referred to as "Americanizers," implemented programs designed to teach English literacy and citizenship skills to anyone identified as "foreign" or otherwise in need of "assimilation" (including, in some cases, native illiterate whites). As immigrant education programs became increasingly standardized, a new class of professional adult educators, based primarily in teachers' colleges, emerged. Throughout the 1920s, these educators gained influence over federal education policy, and their presence on the National Advisory Committee on Illiteracy signaled governmental acceptance of Americanization models as the future of adult education programs.

The debate surrounding the professionalization of literacy education that arose from exchanges between Moonlight Schools supporters and Americanizers remains guiding tropes for discussion surrounding literacy. The virulent public disagreement between the two movements concerning the use of volunteers versus professionally trained teachers to conduct literacy courses was, as the ensuing chapters show, in part responsible for the development of demand for professional literacy educators and researchers and also for a paradoxical lack of respect for literacy teaching as a scholarly endeavor.

The following chapters seek out the historical, rhetorical, and pedagogical conditions and decisions that led to the "failure" of the Moonlight Schools' model of volunteer literacy teaching and to the "success" of the Americaniza-tion-cum–adult education movement's professionalized model of literacy education. I then suggest that the divergent paths of these two movements, despite the "failure" of one and the "success" of the other, succeeded together in shaping our modern discourse surrounding literacy. Because both of these movements have been largely forgotten by educators, chapter 2 provides a historical outline of both movements. Chapter 3 draws on textbooks and ar-chival evidence to illustrate the differing pedagogies employed by each group. I argue that the movements' pedagogies reflect the philosophical differences of the two groups, particularly their conceptions of students' abilities and needs.

Chapter 4 analyzes how the rhetoric of the Moonlight Schools movement shaped and was shaped by the Americanization movement and how both movements presented their educational projects to the American public. In particular, I focus on the intersections of literacy and race in the rhetoric of the two movements. I argue that the Moonlight Schools' invocation of white native identity was made in an effort to appeal to widespread nativist sentiment but that the schools also resisted efforts to paint immigrants as illiterate, ignorant, and unworthy of admission into the United States. The schools' refusal to accept the tenets of Americanization, I assert, ul-timately marginalized the Moonlight Schools within the nascent field of adult education and led to their demise.

Chapter 5 continues my analysis of the intersections between American-ization and the Moonlight Schools by describing the conflict between the

Moonlight Schools' model of volunteer teaching and the Americanization model of professional adult education. The Moonlight Schools continued to forward an image of "teaching writing" as a task that any literate person could perform. To create a professional identity, university-based Americanizers insisted that teaching writing to adults was a difficult undertaking that could only be accomplished by highly trained people conducting lengthy courses. I argue that the Moonlight Schools' volunteer model was rendered unviable thanks to Americanizers' success in establishing a governmental definition of literacy that devalued basic literacy skills and emphasized the necessity of advanced instruction—instruction that only university-trained teachers could provide.

Chapter 6 traces the long-term effects of the exchanges between the Moonlight Schools and Americanizers on public perceptions of literacy education. In tracing these effects, I suggest that we can develop revised and perhaps more effective public representations of the work literacy educators currently undertake.

2. LITERACY, CRISIS, AND
EDUCATIONAL RESPONSES

*L*iteracy as a social ideal is intimately tied to a rhetoric of crisis. The meaning of "literacy" has been defined against its absence: to be literate is to have an ability, a skill, a knowledge that others lack. The *value* of literacy is determined by the social location and volume of this absence; as the site of absence is altered, the cultural capital imputed to literacy is threatened, creating a perception—and a rhetoric—of social crisis. Since the nineteenth century, "value to the community, self- and socioeconomic worth, mobility, access to information and knowledge, rationality, morality, and orderliness are among the many qualities linked to literacy for individuals" (Graff xxxvii). The *absence* of literacy has been perceived as a threat because the absence of literacy also supposedly signals the absence of these qualities: illiteracy has become analogous with irrationality, immorality, a lack of value and economic worth, and a lack of mobility.

Literacy crises were a consistent feature of US social life throughout the twentieth century (and earlier). Between 1900 and 1920, the influx of immigrants from southern and eastern European countries sparked a rhetoric of literacy crisis that painted immigrants as the doom of American democracy. During the same period, the realization that a larger portion of native-born US citizens, particularly in Appalachia, was illiterate sparked a crisis of American identity. In this text, I trace two historical invocations of literacy crisis—the immigrant and Appalachian literacy crises of the early twentieth century—following, in particular, the educative responses to both "events." I select these two events because they represent key moments in the development of public attitudes toward literacy instruction.

In particular, the dialogue between competing literacy educators, I argue, created an environment in which literacy instruction became, for the first time, both a professional field and, paradoxically, an activity that the general public felt empowered to undertake.

Defining "literacy" in terms of one's worth within a given set of social and economic relationships has resulted in an ever-shifting understanding of the term. Deborah Brandt explains: "[A]s with electricity or manufactured goods, individual literacy exists only as part of larger material systems, systems that on one hand enable acts of reading or writing and on the other hand confer their value" (*Literacy* 1). As social structures and economic production have changed, so, too, have the literacy requirements for participation within those socioeconomic systems. In particular, as both the economy and its resulting social structures become increasingly specialized, the need for more complex varieties of literacy has grown. Rhetorics of literacy crisis arise in response to fears that there are too few people who possess the literacy skills necessary to participate in these ever-expanding material systems—either as producers of specialized knowledges and goods or as consumers of those knowledges and goods—but also in response to fears that newly "literate" people may threaten existing social structures. In theory, both producers (and employers) and consumers (and employees) benefit from a relatively egalitarian distribution of literacy skills, because such distribution helps ensure a balance between supply and demand of specialized products. Rhetorics of literacy crisis invoke the demise of equitable distribution—of money, of political power, of social status—as the end result of continued illiteracy. Because of this invocation, literacy crisis rhetorics often draw on tropes of democracy, freedom, and equality and at first blush appear to support equitable, if not altruistic, methods of "correcting" illiterate people.

But the very economic relationships that would seem to demand egalitarian distribution of literacy also create "cycles of competition and change" that "keep raising the stakes for literacy achievement" (Brandt, *Literacy* 2). Though literacy skills "often help to catapult individuals into higher economic brackets and social privilege . . . the very broadening of these abilities among greater numbers of people has enabled economic and technological changes that now destabilize and devalue once serviceable levels of literate skills" (Brandt, *Literacy* 2). In some cases, this devaluation can be read as a process that groups of elites foster as a way to maintain existing power relationships; as Mary Trachsel explains, educational requirements, particularly testing, are "apt to function as mechanisms that enable an educated elite to impose exclusive standards upon academic aspirants" (22). John Trimbur makes much the same argument: "[L]iteracy crises play out in symbolic form the relations between 'ruling groups' and 'popular masses,' as well as the aspirations of the middle class to intellectual, moral, and political leadership" (280). But in other cases, the devaluation of basic literacy skills has less to do with deliberate attempts to retain power and more to do, as Brandt suggests, with the "economic and technological changes" that inevitably result from attempts to produce the very egalitarian distributions of literacy (and power) that are undermined by such changes.

As more people gain access to literate society and the discourses of technology, technologies "improve" in response to the increased demand for those technologies and the increase in knowledgeable workers available to produce them. Though these changes can be read as unmotivated, rather than, as Trachsel and Trimbur would have it, deliberate if unconscious attempts by power groups to maintain status, they nevertheless perpetuate existing class stratification. As members of the underclass gain more literacy skills, the very universality of those skills devalues them: literacy is only valuable if there is an absence against which to measure it. In response to increasingly equitable distribution of literacy skills, new and more complex literacy skills become the new benchmark by which literacy—and the people who have it—are assigned value. Those who already possess socially and economically valued literacy skills have more access to the educational, social, and economic opportunities necessary to "keep up" with the demand for more complex literacies—a position that assures they will *continue* to possess valued literacy skills, even as the measure of "value" becomes increasingly complex and multiple.

Throughout the twentieth century, literacy has often been taken "for granted" (Brandt, *Literacy* 1). When literacy is taken for granted, the power relationships that particular definitions of literacy work to maintain are rendered invisible. I argue that rhetorics of literacy crisis arise when these power relationships are pushed to the forefront by events that force the public to recognize that literacy is not equitably distributed and that literacy is not a skill that can be taken for granted. Rhetorics of literacy crisis thus reflect a social desire to explain and respond to differences in literacy attainment. As Trimbur describes, rhetorics of literacy crisis "perform certain kinds of ideological work by giving a name to and thereby mastering (rhetorically if not actually) cultural anxieties released by demographic shifts, changes in the means of production, new relations and conflicts between classes and groups of people, and reconfigurations of cultural hegemony" (286). As Trimbur, Michael R. Olneck, and Ira Shor have separately argued, perceived literacy crises have less to do with actual literacy attainment and more to do with threats to social identity—in particular, threats to middle-class economic opportunity or, I argue, threats to the belief that middle-class economic opportunities are products of middle-class values (such as hard work, thrift, cleanliness, dedication to education) and, as such, equally available to all people.

Rhetorics of literacy crisis perform ideological work not only by *explaining* differences between people(s)—what Trimbur terms "giving a name to . . . cultural anxieties" (286)—but also by *excusing* and *eliminating* differences in (perceived) literacy attainment. Literacy crises function not only to mark particular populations as deficient but also to explain how these deficiencies came to exist and to eradicate the threat posed by difference. In particular, literacy crises work to reify the narrative that economic opportunities (and, concomitantly, educational success) are awarded on a meritocratic basis: in short, that those who have power, status, or money have earned it. That is, literacy crises respond to ruptures in the US narrative of equal opportunity by working to make invisible, once more, the power relationships that literacy works to maintain.

Literacy crises tend to follow similar rhetorical patterns. Following an initial "revelation" of the crisis, critics seek to place blame for the crisis both on those who "lack" literacy and on the social structures that have permitted this lack, simultaneously celebrating the importance of "literacy" to socioeconomic development. Organizational structures (social, institutional, and/or economic) are developed to transfer the missing literacy skills to the lacking population. These structures can be read as providing a way for the "literate" to absolve themselves of guilt for the unequal economic and social-class status they enjoy based on their literate status—hence, "solutions" offered to literacy crises are often characterized by appeals to benevolence, kindness, altruism, and social responsibility. Although literacy crises often share these beginnings, what happens next—how these skills are accepted by the "illiterate," how social structures respond to this newly literate public, and what becomes of the organizational structures—varies widely from crisis to crisis. In the remainder of this chapter, I trace two responses to the interrelated Appalachian and immigrant literacy crises that erupted in the first two decades of the twentieth century.

History of the Moonlight Schools

The first Moonlight Schools were held on September 4, 1911, in Rowan County, Kentucky. The schools were organized by county school super-intendent Cora Wilson Stewart, who, in her later speeches and published works, explains that she was inspired to create a program of adult education through encounters with three local people who could not read and write and who she felt embodied the "classes" of people who were not literate: "mothers, separated from their absent children," "middle-aged men, shut out form the world of books," and "youths and maidens who possessed rare talents" (*Moonlight Schools: . . . Illiterates* 13). Florence S. Estes, however, demonstrates that while these encounters with specific illiterate people likely did spur Stewart to action, Stewart was aware of regional and national educational movements, including the Conference for Education in the South and the country life movement, that sought to improve the lives of southern agricultural workers through education (18; 46–67). While the Moonlight Schools were designed to serve Stewart's local community, the curriculum Stewart created owed much to the ethos of the country life movement, particularly its emphasis on "scientific agriculture" and the "modernization of infrastructures of commerce, such as banks, roads, and credit systems" (Estes 47). Hence, though the primary focus of the Moonlight Schools was to eliminate illiteracy, the schools welcomed all adult students because Stewart believed all could benefit from additional education.

The Moonlight Schools were unique, however, in attempting to teach basic literacy skills to native-born adults. The Conference on Education in the South and the country life movement both advocated improved education systems, but these improvements were directed at childhood education and at agricultural education for literate adults. Adults who had not attained basic skills were viewed as essentially uneducable. Stewart created the Moonlight Schools on the premise that adults were, in fact, easily taught and, more important, that the act of teaching adults would ultimately further the goals of improving childhood education. She argues that "the influence which such schools [as the Moonlight Schools] exert in bringing [adults] in sympathy with the cause" of compulsory education would make the schools worthwhile; she suggests that "if the effort is not worth making for [adults'] sake, it surely is worth making for the sake of their children. We are convinced that by this means that [*sic*] we can better convert parents and overcome their indifference and antagonism, and can make of them what we must have if we succeed even in educating the youth—friends and advocates of the school" (Untitled speech 14).

If adults could be convinced of the value of education, they would be more likely to support practical improvements to school buildings, remedying the "poorly heated, poorly lighted, poorly ventilated" schoolroom that often characterized rural education (De Garmo 304). Stewart cites several examples of such improvements: One man explains that after the Moonlight Schools arrived, "we papered the [school]house, put in new windows, purchased new stovepipe, made new steps, contributed money, and bought the winter's fuel," while others were inspired to "build new steps, put up hemstitched curtains and paint the school-house besides" (*Moonlight Schools: . . . Illiterates* 45, 24). The Moonlight Schools, Stewart argued, could also improve the quality of rural teaching. Not only would the parents be more likely to demand qualified teachers if they understood the value of education but teachers themselves could also receive additional training through Moonlight Schools' institutes. Though these institutes focused on "the methods of teaching adult illiterates, materials to use, ways and means of reaching the stubborn and getting them into school and other things relative to the problem of educating adults" (*Moonlight Schools: . . . Illiterates* 32), many of the discussions would have had applicability to children's education, particularly the importance of providing reading material relevant to students' lives and interests.

Like the supporters of the country life movement and the wider progressive movement throughout the country, Stewart suggested that "social institutions needed to be developed in the countryside" (Estes 50). It was, after all, the lack of such institutions that had created an illiterate student population in need of Moonlight Schools. Providing adults with educational opportunity was the best way to create a sense of community that would promote the development of social institutions. As Stewart argued before the World Conference on Education, teaching adults to read and write "means paving the way for religion, mutual understanding and good will, trade relations and most other things that affect the lives of men and women and of nations" ("World Conference" 4). One of the explicit benefits Stewart outlines is a "whetted desire for cooperative activity where individualism and stagnation had prevailed. Friction and factional feeling melted away in districts where they had existed, and a new spirit of harmony and brotherhood came to take their place" (*Moonlight Schools: . . . Illiterates* 45–46).

Stewart believed that if adult education could bring such benefits, it should be as widely available as possible—in fact, adult education opportunities should be as widespread as childhood education and should be available concomitantly. Many speeches in support of the Moonlight Schools climaxed with this parallel, for instance:

> A day school in every community! Once it was a doubtful experiment, and it has come up through trials and tribulations innumerable. But now it is an established institution. A night school in every community! If a cultivated community, for more culture: for specialization. If an illiterate community, for their emancipation from illiteracy, and their new birth into the realms of knowledge and power. ("Moonlight Schools" 14)

Stewart suggested that neglecting education for adults was impractical and, worse, unchristian. She asserted that "the public school should be as liberal in its policy as is the Church. I do not believe that it has any right to say to men and women, 'If you embrace me not before a certain hour, or before a certain age, I will close my doors to you forever!'" (14). Furthermore, educating illiterates simply made economic and social sense: men and women who had half their working lives ahead of them would be better workers—less apt to waste time or to damage machinery because they could not read operating instructions—if they could read and write.

METHODS AND DISSEMINATION

Before the Moonlight Schools could begin, Stewart needed to convince adults to attend. Stewart's background played an essential role in her success. She was born and raised in Rowan County, her father a respected doctor, and her brother a local politician. She had worked as a teacher and held the elected office of superintendent. Her community knew that she had shown deep care for the community and respect for its members, and her appeals—both to volunteers to teach and students to enroll—were especially persuasive because she could point to her previous successful work as an educator to substantiate her claims. Indeed, even Stewart's heartbreaking past—her divorce from an abusive husband and the death of her young son—played to her advantage. Although Stewart never explicitly referenced these events, even to close friends, everyone in her hometown was aware of them, and they are often referred to obliquely in letters from her early Moonlight Schools work. These events rendered Stewart human, establishing her identity in such a way that she was not perceived as "talking down" to those who needed the schools most, as settlement workers often were. Furthermore, Stewart's experiences as superintendent taught her how to organize her teaching corps in effective ways to reach all potential students.

Stewart enlisted volunteers to "visit each home in the district and issue a personal invitation to every adult in Rowan County" (Baldwin 42). Based on the feedback volunteers received, Stewart estimated that 150 students would attend the first session. Instead, the first Moonlight Schools session enrolled 1,200 students of all ages (*Moonlight Schools: . . . Illiterates* 16). The courses "met Monday through Thursday evenings from seven to nine o'clock for six weeks. Sessions began promptly at seven. . . . Students left promptly at nine" (Baldwin 44). Coursework focused on reading and writing with additional elective drills in other subjects (including math, history, and speech). Stewart asked that every student who completed the course write her a letter, and she used the letters to signify graduation from the schools. If the students had been illiterate, this letter signified their attainment of literacy. Thus, Stewart defined "literacy" as the ability to write a simple letter and to read the material assigned during the first course of the Moonlight Schools. However, many of the enrollees were not illiterates; most were adults who had not had the opportunity to complete their education or who wished to improve particular skills. For instance, Stewart relates the story of one man who "specialized in mathematics" to improve his work at a lumber camp and who received a promotion at the end of his six-week session (*Moonlight Schools: . . . Illiterates* 38).

Following the first session, Stewart held the first Moonlight Schools institute, designed as a place for teachers to exchange methods and information. At the institute, teachers pointed out that the goal of eliminating illiteracy could not be achieved through school-based learning alone; many illiterates could not attend schools due to poor roads, poor health, and childcare responsibilities. Furthermore, teachers had no real sense of how many illiterates were present in their districts. US Census data provided some basis for estimates, but teachers did not have access to the names of illiterates in their districts, and the government's method for determining literacy status was suspect. In response to these critiques, Stewart organized the teachers to conduct a census of adults throughout the county. Teachers once again visited adults and this time took notes regarding literacy skills as well as personality, employment, relationships, and, perhaps most important, potential ways to motivate each adult to attend the schools. With this data in hand, Stewart encouraged all literate people to seek out illiterates and teach them. She enlisted doctors to teach their patients, employers to teach their employees, and children to teach their parents. In addition, many teachers sought out illiterates in their districts and offered home instruction. By the end of the third Moonlight Schools sessions, Stewart calculated that "only twenty-three illiterates remained in the county" (Baldwin 46).

Stewart's idea gained immediate national attention. By December 1911, less than four months after the inauguration of the schools, Stewart gave a speech about the Moonlight Schools to the Southern Educational Association in Houston, Texas. The next year, Stewart "spoke to the state educational associations of Alabama, Arkansas, Virginia, and South Carolina" (Nelms 41) and "embarked on a statewide promotional campaign" (Baldwin 49). By the end of 1913, Moonlight Schools were active throughout Kentucky. In addition, P. P. Claxton, US Commissioner of Education, published a special bulletin, "Illiteracy in the United States and an Experiment for Its Elimination," that touted the Moonlight Schools as one possible solution to the national problem of adult illiteracy. The Moonlight Schools, he suggests, demonstrate "that it is not so difficult for illiterate grown-ups to learn to read and write as is generally supposed" and that "adults of limited education have taken advantage of the opportunity to return to school and to increase their knowledge" (qtd. in US Cong., House, Committee on Education 57). Using statistics from the 1910 census, the bulletin also demonstrates "that illiteracy was not solely a southern problem" (Baldwin 51). In doing so, the bulletin created a nationwide audience for the Moonlight Schools.

In Kentucky, Stewart petitioned the state government to create an agency that could oversee and support the Moonlight Schools. To overcome the objections of legislators who believed that illiteracy was limited to the mountain region, Stewart convinced the census bureau "to give her the names of Kentucky illiterates, listed by county of residence" (*Moonlight Schools: . . . Illiterates* 52). The census bureau reports convinced legislators—or rather, their constituents—that illiteracy was indeed a statewide problem, and the state government agreed to create the Kentucky Illiteracy Commission (KIC) in February 1914. However, the state appropriated no money to the KIC, which was funded instead through donations. Most of these donations were from Kentucky clubwomen; Yvonne Honeycutt Baldwin finds that the Kentucky Federation of Women's Clubs donated "more than $34,000" to the KIC (59). It was through donations from Kentucky clubwomen that the KIC staged its first big event, Illiteracy Week, in November 1914. The event accomplished Stewart's goal of publicizing the extent of illiteracy in Kentucky and the effectiveness of the Moonlight Schools; Peter Mortensen calculates that in Lexington, Kentucky, alone, newspapers published thirty articles about Illiteracy Week (9).

The KIC's success in drawing attention and funding to adult literacy education programs inspired other states to create illiteracy commissions, including, in the order in which the states developed commissions, South Carolina, North Carolina, Mississippi, Arkansas, New Mexico, Alabama, and Oklahoma (Nelms; Baldwin). Federated clubwomen also began statewide Moonlight Schools' programs in Kansas, Minnesota, and Wisconsin (Nelms; Baldwin). However, the KIC was less successful in providing concrete support to active Moonlight Schools in Kentucky. The KIC did hire three "county agents" who worked with local superintendents to organize a comprehensive Moonlight Schools programs in their assigned counties, but because Stewart was totally dependent on volunteer funds, she was able to offer little more than moral support to the thousands of Kentucky educators working in Moonlight Schools.

When the KIC's initial mandate ended in 1916, Stewart requested that the legislature renew the commission until 1920, because the KIC's stated goal was to eliminate illiteracy prior to the 1920 census, and provide a $20,000 appropriation to fund the commission's work. Many members of the government, including the governor, felt that Kentucky's meager government funds would be better spent on day school education but did dole out half of the fund requested: $10,000 for 1916 and 1917 (Baldwin 83). Though the legislature passed a bill "requiring school trustees to take a census of adult illiterates," it provided no funding for the work (Baldwin 84). While the KIC could hire more county illiteracy agents with its new funds, the commission continued to require volunteer donations to provide Moonlight Schools with materials.

In part to assuage the difficulties overworked local teachers faced in preparing materials and in part to promote the vision of rural improvement invoked by the country life movement, Stewart composed a set of primers, *The Country Life Readers*, designed specifically for rural adult students. In one sense, *The Country Life Readers* put an additional financial burden on the Moonlight Schools movement—as a published, bound text, the books cost more to produce than the simple newspapers that teachers had previously prepared. However, many of the proceeds from the books were returned to Stewart in royalties, and she funneled these funds back into her illiteracy work. Moreover, the books made it much easier for volunteers, saving teachers' time and encouraging more people to volunteer for Moonlight Schools work.

FROM LOCAL WORK TO A NATIONAL MOVEMENT

By 1917, Moonlight Schools were active in many states. However, though connected by a shared vision and pedagogical stance, Moonlight Schools' programs functioned as isolated regional efforts. With few exceptions, schools were organized only in areas where illiteracy had *already* been a public issue, especially in the South and in areas where illiteracy was attributed to particular minority groups (for instance, Native Americans in Minnesota, African Americans in Alabama, Spanish speakers in New Mexico). Despite Stewart's success in rallying individual state governments to provide education for illiterates, her movement had not yet moved to the national stage.

US entry into World War I proved to be the necessary impetus for bringing the Moonlight Schools to national attention. In 1917, the US Army began to administer an IQ test to enlistees. Brandt explains that two different versions of the text existed: "the Alpha (a standard pencil-and-paper test) and the Beta (a combination of pictures, oral instructions, and gestures)" ("Drafting" 490). One-third of enlistees took the Beta test, and seven hundred thousand signed by mark ("Drafting" 491); in Kentucky, thirty thousand men signed by mark (Baldwin 109). Moreover, a great many of these men were native born. These figures shocked the nation and particularly its educators—the National Education Association's (NEA) *Journal of Addresses and Proceedings* for 1917, 1918, and 1919 are filled with references to the "army tests" and the failure of the education system that the tests (supposedly) illustrated. Stewart used the army's findings to begin a campaign urging literate people to seek out and instruct drafted soldiers, and she composed a special reader, *The Soldier's First Book*, for use in the army camp schools of the Young Men's Christian Association (YMCA). The YMCA also "purchased sixty thousand . . . *Country Life Readers* to use in camp schools across the country" (Baldwin 104). Though the YMCA did not organize Moonlight Schools per se, the widespread use of Stewart's books among soldiers ensured that her name became indelibly associated with literacy education.

More important, the test's "discovery" of high levels of illiteracy among native-born people reconfigured public perceptions of illiteracy. Before the war, illiteracy had often been imagined as a disease quarantined among the foreign born (in the urban North) and African Americans and Appalachians (in the rural South). The army tests demonstrated that illiterates hailed from all areas of the country and were not limited to any social, ethnic, or racial group. The tests nationalized illiteracy. In response, the Moonlight Schools also became a national cause. Because the Moonlight Schools offered a broadly aimed program that had been used successfully to educate a variety of groups—native whites, African Americans, Native Americans, and, to a lesser extent, non-English speakers—many educators and public officials saw the Moonlight Schools as a cheap and effective way to eliminate the illiteracy problem.

The Kentucky legislature likewise turned to the Moonlight Schools as a solution to the illiteracy revealed among the state's draftees. But while Kentucky aptly reflects the newfound willingness of government officials to fund literacy efforts, it also demonstrates the dangers of Stewart's campaign rhetoric. Stewart had based her appeals for KIC funding on the premise that if adequately funded, the KIC could eliminate illiteracy before the 1920 census. The Kentucky legislature granted Stewart's premise and, inspired by the revelations of the army test, appropriated $75,000 ($25,000 per year in 1918, 1919, and 1920) to the KIC (Baldwin 112). After 1920, the KIC "would cease to exist" (113). Either the Moonlight Schools would fulfill their mission, or they would prove themselves a failure—but in either case, the schools would not be entitled to further governmental support.

Although Stewart calculated that 130,000 of Kentucky's 200,000 illiterates had learned to write through the Moonlight Schools, the 1920 census found that 155,004 illiterates remained in the state. We have no way to accurately document how many people "became literate" through Moonlight

Schools education: teachers often varied in the criteria used to designate students as "illiterate," and not all schools reported to Stewart. Nor can we rely on census data to determine the number of illiterates, because the system used by census officials to determine illiteracy was equally vague and unreliable. It is perhaps safe to assume that the number of students who learned to read and write in the Moonlight Schools lies somewhere between the figures Stewart presented and the census figures; while the schools may not have reached as many "absolute illiterates" as Stewart claimed, it seems likely that the schools educated more people than the census would suggest. Even if we accept the census report as accurate, the Moonlight Schools' largest student population was not illiterates but men and women who had begun their education and, for a variety of reasons, had been unable to finish.

The Kentucky legislature did not wait for census data. In 1920, Kentucky discontinued funding for the KIC, under pressure from school officials who perceived (incorrectly) that the KIC's funding would be reappropriated to day-school education. In fact, the legislature cut funding for all types of education (Baldwin 119).[1] Though the end of the KIC was a setback for the schools, ultimately, the demise of the KIC likely encouraged the schools' national spread. Although Stewart had refused several offers to join national organizations because she felt her duty lay with Kentucky, her disgust with the state government freed her to take her work to a national audience.

To reach a larger audience, Stewart began writing a guidebook to the Moonlight Schools: *Moonlight Schools: For the Emancipation of Adult Illiterates*, published in 1922. The guide presented a brief history of the movement, the basic ideological premises of the Moonlight Schools, guidance about how best to begin a school, sample texts from students, and pedagogical tips. Stewart could not visit every location that needed a Moonlight School; even if such a feat had been possible for a single individual, Stewart was short of money and often could not afford to travel unless her audiences could pay her travel expenses. Therefore, *Moonlight Schools* acted as a proxy for Stewart herself, carrying both the message and the methods of the schools to far-flung corners of the nation.

Stewart's newfound national following led to a series of opportunities to address an even broader public. In 1918, Stewart was asked to lead the NEA's Illiteracy Committee. This post provided Stewart with an annual platform from which to address the nation's teachers and to rally them to the cause of educating illiterates. Stewart was also asked to "second the nomination of... James B. Cox for president of the United States" in 1920, and she gave an extended speech to the Democratic National Convention (Baldwin 127). Later, at the 1923 World Conference on Education, Stewart led discussion concerning illiteracy. During the event, the Moonlight Schools gained international recognition as a potential solution to illiteracy, and educators in England and Russia in particular long sought Stewart's advice in conducting literacy campaigns. Stewart also arranged a number of regional and national literacy conferences, events that brought together leading theorists and activists to discuss the best methods for eliminating and preventing illiteracy.

Increasingly, however, Stewart found that advocates of Americanization programs received the lion's share of attention both among NEA members and at the literacy conferences Stewart helped to organize. Stewart disagreed with Americanizers on many points (see chapter 4), but she was particularly incensed by the fact that educational programs for the foreign-born were liberally funded by many state and local governments while she struggled to locate minimal funding for illiteracy programs targeting the native-born. In keeping with this trend, Stewart's NEA Illiteracy Commission was merged with the NEA Department of Immigrant Education in 1925 to create the Department of Adult Education. However, Stewart refused to give up her autonomy—and particularly her control over her commission's funds—because she feared that the department would push aside the problems of native-born and absolute illiterates in favor of concerns related to foreign-born and semiliterate people.

Stewart responded to the merge by creating a new organization that would specifically target native-born and absolute illiterates: the National Illiteracy Crusade (NIC). To ensure that the organization would garner immediate attention from clubwomen and philanthropic organizations, Stewart filled the crusade's board of directors with well-known activists, including Jane Addams, Ida Tarbell, and Carrie Chapman Catt (Baldwin 165). Though her choices did achieve a high level of name recognition for the organization, not all of the attention was positive. The Daughters of the American Revolution, for example, refused to support Moonlight Schools' efforts because its members believed that Stewart and her crusade were tacitly supporting communism (because they perceived Addams and Catt as supporting bolshevism) (Baldwin 167). Accusations of communist sympathy certainly worked against the NIC, but the organization had more pressing problems. With the passage of restrictive immigration laws in 1917 and 1921, public concern about illiteracy began to wane. Despite the momentary peak of recognition for native illiteracy sparked by the army tests, many people assumed that continuing illiteracy was a product of immigration; when immigration was limited and a literacy test was required for entrance into the United States, interest in remedying the "immigrant problem" slowly decreased. By 1925, both Americanizers and Stewart had much more difficulty locating funding for literacy education projects.

In spite of its shoestring budget, the NIC did achieve some of Stewart's goals. In 1929, the organization published *Mother's First Book*, a primer designed for illiterate women who could not attend regular Moonlight Schools classes. Focusing primarily on childcare, the text was designed not only to improve the literacy abilities of women but also to improve their ability to care for their children; the text included lessons on eating habits, hygiene, and childhood education. The Metropolitan Life Insurance Company agreed to publicize the book, and several organizations agreed to pay for its publication (Baldwin 171). The NIC also brought increased attention to illiteracy among Native Americans, and the Bureau of Indian Affairs began Moonlight Schools classes for Native Americans.

These accomplishments, though, were not enough for Stewart. In 1929, she convinced President Herbert Hoover to appoint the National Advisory Committee on Illiteracy (NACI). Stewart had hoped that the organization would have the benefit of federal support, but she was disappointed: though Hoover offered the government's resources, he allocated no funding to the organization. Furthermore, the NACI's membership—appointed by the secretary of the interior—was made up of both Stewart's supporters and former Americanization advocates. The Americanizers argued that adult education encapsulated more than basic literacy instruction, and they believed that teachers of adults should be trained professionals, not volunteers. Throughout her time with the NACI, former Americanizers constantly thwarted Stewart in her attempts to promote Moonlight Schools' work. The vision of adult education the NACI promulgated was one of extensive, professionally taught courses, a substantially different vision than the philosophy espoused by the Moonlight Schools.

Though the NACI did manage to publish an instruction manual for teachers of adults—a manual that entirely reflected a professionalized view of adult education rather than Stewart's volunteer-oriented approach—the government's refusal to provide funding guaranteed that whatever the vision of the NACI, little could be accomplished toward its goals. Locating funding became even more difficult as the Depression set in. The organization was all but defunct by 1932 and was officially closed in January 1933. As the NACI declined, so, too, did the Moonlight Schools movement it was intended to represent. Though Stewart continued to publicize the schools for an additional year, new government programs that offered literacy education undercut her message. In 1935, Stewart retired from her work with education to pursue a religious calling, and with her retirement, the Moonlight Schools movement faded away.

Americanization: A Brief History

As Bernard J. Weiss and Robert A. Carlson have both outlined, Americanization education can be defined in a variety of ways. Carlson defines as Americanizers those who "sought to uphold freedom by indoctrinating norms of belief in religion, politics, and economics" (4). By this definition, Americanization can be said to predate the formation of the United States as a country. Alternatively, Weiss draws on Ellwood Cubberley to define Americanization as the effort to "assimilate and amalgamate these people [the immigrants] as part of our American race, and to implant in their children, so far as can be done, the Anglo-Saxon conception of righteousness, law and order, and popular government" (xiii). Throughout this text, the term "Americanization" refers to programs or classes (formal or informal) that aimed to teach immigrants civic values, as well as to the organizations and propaganda that supported those classes. I use the relatively broad term "civic values" to cover a variety of lessons, including English language teaching, citizenship education, and trade education (because trade education also taught a particular set of behaviors associated with middle-class values, including timeliness and thrift). Also, the time frame is 1900 to 1935.

Many different agencies, clubs, and individuals organized Americanization courses. Groups who otherwise had little in common shared an interest in assimilating immigrants. In addition to a general sense of patriotism, this shared interest was largely pragmatic: "unassimilated" immigrants represented a potentially decisive force in local and national politics and industries. Those groups who could attract immigrants to their cause significantly increased their organizational clout and, in the case of businesses, their economic position. As one of the most prominent Americanizers, Frances Kellor, explained in 1919: "If I cannot sell [Americanization] to you as a good business proposition, it simply will not become a reality in this country" (35).

Just as Kellor suggests, businesses organized some of the earliest and most well-known examples of Americanization courses to instruct workers, in recognition of the economic benefits of such instruction. Many business owners believed that literacy education would improve efficiency and safety, while English fluency would simplify the process of distributing safety material to workers. For instance, as Gerd Korman explains, the chairman of the National Safety Council, J. B. Douglas, pointed out that labor laws that had "required foremen overseeing hazardous work to speak the language of their workers" were in many cases impractical, given the diversity of most factory workforces (154); the director of the US Board of Vocational Education, Charles A. Prosser, "agreed that safety bulletins could 'be made a very practical drill in English'" (qtd. in Korman 155). If safety notices and instructions could be printed in a common language, employers could more easily ensure the safety of both their workers and the companies' (often expensive) equipment.

Little biographical information exists concerning individual Americanization advocates, but most prominent organizers seem to have been inspired to pursue Americanization by experiences in other fields. Kellor, for instance, worked as a lawyer and sociologist and focused on labor issues, which brought her into contact with immigrants who Kellor recognized were often taken advantage of because of their unfamiliarity with the English language and American culture (Partridge 18). Similarly, industrialists who sponsored classes were motivated first by a desire to improve efficiency but also, somewhat less cynically, by a desire to improve what they perceived to be immigrants' poor quality of living. Unlike the Moonlight Schools, which by all accounts were inspired primarily by Stewart's identification with people in her community, then, Americanization advocates were most often inspired by recognition of difference, by the awareness of a lack of community among workers and between workers and employers.

The most well-known Americanization program was run by Henry Ford. In 1914, the Ford Motor Company announced a five-dollar-per-day wage for workers, a remarkable sum for manual labor at the time. However, the wage was not without conditions. Many feared that immigrants were not competent to decide how to spend this windfall: one sociologist asked, "[W]ill they live still in the same dirt and squalor . . . to spend more money in a way that will not benefit them or society?" (qtd. in Nevins 553). Company investigators visited homes to determine workers' marital status, economic position, and lifestyle (553–54); men (and later women) were required to "prove that they were 'sober, saving, steady, industrious'" (552) to qualify for the maximum salary. Non-English-speaking workers were also required to enroll in the company's English school or face dismissal (552–54).

Though certainly a charitable element was in company's efforts to educate and oversee workers, the requirements for higher pay also effectively ensured a quality workforce: if all workers spoke English, the company could streamline operations, while "sober" and "industrious" workers were likely to work hard and show up on time. On the demand side of Ford's economic equation, "saving" workers were potential consumers of Ford's products or, if not direct buyers, contributors to establishing a viable local economy. Because of the Ford's position as the most visible company in the country, as well as its leading role in an exponentially expanding industry, Ford's decision to engage in Americanization work set the tone and model for other large industries around the country.

Ford coordinated with the YMCA to design and run English school courses with help from company volunteers and materials purchased with company funds. This model was not unusual: the YMCA became a leading source for Americanization courses and pedagogies. The organization coordinated with industries to provide materials and methods for industry-based classes—as with the United Steel Company in 1913 (McBride 150)—or to actually run courses whose teachers and supplies were paid for by companies, as in the case of Ford Motor. The federal government entered into such an agreement with the YMCA to educate enlisted men immediately before, during, and after World War I. The YMCA's special secretary for immigrant affairs, Peter Roberts, became a leading pedagogical theorist for the Americanization movement, creating the "Roberts method" of instruction, which, like the Moonlight Schools' pedagogies, emphasized the need for vocabulary and reading lessons that addressed the specific experiences of the immigrant students (McBride).

Businesses were not alone in competing for immigrant workers' time and loyalties. Trade unions were active in recruiting immigrant membership and in educating immigrants in English and in pro-labor ideologies.

Wendy Sharer, for instance, has outlined the work of the Women's Trade Union League (WTUL) to develop narratives for teaching English to immigrant workers. The proceedings of the WTUL's annual convention speak to the existence of and demand for union-based Americanization courses; in 1909, one convention speaker explains that "with reference to the English classes which the New York League has started . . . we have had large demand for the classes and for regular teachers" (New York League 17). While industry-based programs were often tacitly or explicitly required for workers, union programs operated on voluntary basis. Organizers attempted to attract students by pointing out the valuable bargaining power that students could gain through English fluency; as the WTUL points out, "some [workers] were under-paid because they could not understand English and could not read the agreements in the shops" (Hennessy 46).

Other public and private organizations were also active in Americanization projects, each emphasizing its own particular brand of American identity. The General Federation of Women's Clubs (GFWC), for instance, bolstered its own ranks and increased recognition of women's importance to the nation by targeting immigrant women with Americanization programs. These programs included staged pageants on patriotic themes (see White), informal efforts to befriend immigrant women, and direct instruction. For instance, the chairwoman for education at the GFWC, Helen Varick Boswell, exhorts the membership to "organize for them [immigrant women], as has been done in a number of places, classes from two to three in the afternoon" (206). She argues that clubs should also "organize mothers' classes, cooking classes, sewing classes, and classes for entertainment" (206). In 1916, the GFWC, "by vote, decided to stress . . . The Immigrant Problem and Americanization" (Winter 3). In one case, California's branch of the GFWC allowed the state Department of Education to prepare a bulletin on the issue of "national unity, particularly as affected by education" (California Commission 60). Many clubwomen understood their work as improving society; because immigrants were among the most visible and widely discussed social "problems" of the era, clubwomen engaged in Americanization as a way to fulfill their civic responsibilities—and in doing so, emphasized that women were the cornerstones of patriotic society.

The outbreak of World War I acted as a unifying force for the nascent Americanization movement. While methods and motives still varied widely, the war established a consistent rhetorical call to arms that served not only to attract volunteers (and paid employees) but also funds for more classes and more materials: a call that framed immigrants as actual threats to American democracy but that displaced this threat onto immigrants' literacy rather than confronting directly the prejudices against particular religious and national groups. Because "illiteracy" and not "immigration" was marked as the problem, immigrants' education was a matter of national and cultural security. The *Addresses and Proceedings* of the NEA's annual meeting aptly demonstrates the tenor of this rhetoric. One educator writes, "No democracy can be safe or efficient when more than five million of its people are illiterate" (Coffman 168). Another argues, "[I]lliteracy must be obliterated, ignorance must vanish, before the people can constitute a real democracy" (Driver 65); and yet another claims, "Insisting that our democracy shall be kept safe for the world, we demand resolute, sustained measures that shall eradicate illiteracy from all sections of the country. The complete Americanization of all native- and foreign-born residents is the paramount duty of the hour" (Department of Superintendence 489).

Perhaps not surprising, the outbreak of World War I in Europe and the depiction of immigrant education as a matter of national "safety" spurred governmental agencies to take a more direct role in creating and sustaining Americanization programs. At the local level, city governments appropriated funds and directly organized courses for immigrant residents. Cleveland, for instance, not only commissioned Americanization programs but also organized a survey to analyze the "problem" of immigrants and the success or failure of particular methods of Americanization (see Miller). The Bureau of Naturalization records that by 1922, 3,016 communities requested information related to designing Americanization programs (McClymer, "Americanization"). Similarly, many state governments, particularly in New England and the Midwest, oversaw and appropriated funds for public evening schools.

While city councils could appropriate funds directly to carry out Americanization efforts, the federal government—while equally invested in the project of assimilation—was hindered by a long-standing sentiment that education was the province of the states. Indeed, the Bureau of Naturalization was specifically instructed not to set aside funds for the support of Americanization courses (McClymer, "Americanization"). Instead, the bureau supported Americanization courses through the publication of textbooks and teacher-training guides and by providing the data local

Literacy, Crisis, and Educational Responses

communities requested. Likewise, the armed forces coordinated with the YMCA to provide on-base instruction to illiterate enlistees; though many of the illiterates were, in fact, native-born white men, the program was frequently imagined and described as an Americanization program (see Thorngate).

The bureaucratizing of Americanization programs, perhaps more than any other single event, led to the professionalization of Americanization efforts. The agencies that appropriated money to Americanization programs demanded proof that their funds were being used appropriately; between 1916 and 1925, local and national studies had been conducted to determine whether Americanization courses were successful in educating and assimilating immigrants (see Miller; Thompson). In almost every case, the published results document poor teaching, poor student retention, and little actual learning. Nearly every leading figure within Americanization, including surveyors Frank Thompson and Herbert Miller, educational theorist Peter Roberts, and Bureau of Naturalization chief John Mahoney, called for the development of professional training programs for Americanization teachers. Although teacher training was perceived as a necessity for the continued success of the Americanization movement, changes in immigration law called this relationship into question.

THE TRANSFORMATION OF AMERICANIZERS

The success of Americanizers' efforts to create immigrant illiteracy as a threat to national security and subsequent government interest in immigrant education led to the 1917 passage of a law requiring incoming immigrants to pass a literacy test. Efforts to institute a literacy test began in 1891; though measures passed both houses of Congress five times, all were subject to presidential veto. That the law was finally passed over Woodrow Wilson's veto in 1917 speaks both to increasing anti-European sentiment sparked by the war and, perhaps more important, the success of campaigns to paint illiteracy as a national threat.

Despite its significance in signaling a new federal outlook on immigrants and immigration, the literacy test did relatively little to actually exclude incoming immigrants. Claudia Goldin and Gary Libecap find that in 1917, the first year in which illiterates were subject to exclusion, fines (and presumably deportation orders) were levied against only 192 incoming immigrants (out of almost 300,000) (226).[2] A wide variety of exceptions were built into the law, including immigrants avoiding religious persecution and immigrants arriving to join family members in the United States. Moreover, additional exceptions were made: the commissioner of immigration in 1919, for instance, complained that "the exceptions made to the illiteracy test (as a war measure) in favor of laborers coming from Mexico have so modified conditions on the southern border that a fair estimate can hardly be made as to what the effect of the test would have been there under normal conditions" (US Department of Labor, *Annual Report* [1919], 15). In 1933, another immigration commissioner calculated that admissions of illiterate people who were exempted from the literacy test made up 2.2 percent of the 4,944,743 immigrants admitted between 1917 and 1933 (MacCormack, letter to Stewart).

As an exclusionary tool, then, the literacy test for immigrant admission was highly unsuccessful. As a rhetorical tool for galvanizing public concern about immigrant illiteracy, the test was an immense success. Hence, Americanization programs gained far more publicity, if not more actual participants, *after* the passage of the literacy test. Moreover, as John Hennen and John Higham have separately argued, the "defensive posture" taken by the United States as a whole in the immediate postwar years further heightened the perception of immigrants—especially those who were imagined as unable to participate in US social and political institutions—as threats to society (Hennen 119). Between 1917 and 1925, Americanization programs appear to have thrived. The NEA's *Addresses and Proceedings* again indicate prevailing trends: throughout the period, each year brings an increasing number of talks addressing Americanization efforts and, in 1921, the formation of a Department of Immigrant Education.

But another event occurred in 1921 that signaled the end of the Americanization movement: the passage of the Emergency Immigration Act. This act, like the rise of Americanization programs, was an instantiation of the generally isolationist stance adopted by the United States in the wake of World War I. The Emergency Immigration Act maintained many of the provisions of the 1917 Immigration Act, including the literacy test, but added a new policy for restriction. The act states: "the number of aliens of any nationality who may be admitted under the immigration laws to the United States in any fiscal year shall be limited to 3 per centum of the number of foreign-born persons of such nationality resident in the United States as determined by the United States census of 1910" (United States, Dept. of

Labor, *Annual Report* [1921], 16). Though the bill, as its name implies, was intended to be a temporary stopgap measure to staunch the overwhelming flow of immigrants, the quota system, with many modifications, remains in effect today.

The effects of the quota system of Americanization programs were not immediate, but two long-term changes ultimately curbed the rhetorical efficacy of Americanizers' appeals. First, the quota system drastically reduced the number of immigrants arriving each year. Previously, the sheer volume of immigrants in a given year set the stage for the rhetoric of threat favored by Americanizers: by numbers alone, the immigrants represented a potential threat to current political arrangements as well as "native" jobs and access to social services. When the number of immigrants dropped significantly, Americanizers found it difficult to maintain this sense of impending threat. The less visible immigrants became, the less willing natives were to donate their time and energies to educating them. Second, the Americanizers' own rhetorical efforts undermined their long-term viability. Many Americans took the Americanizers at their word: if their programs taught children and adults to read and write effectively and if immigration had slowed to a relative trickle, the problem of immigrant illiteracy, the general public assumed, must have been largely rectified by the mid- and late 1920s. Though Americanization programs continue to exist today (see Salomone), the programs targeted to second-wave immigrants were largely defunct by 1930.

The decline in demand for Americanization programs and Americanization teachers created an employment problem: teachers who had spent time (and often money) completing professionalization programs designed for teachers of immigrants were left with no outlet for their expertise. More influentially, the people who had demanded and developed those professionalization programs were likewise unable to justify their professional positions. I argue that it was this certification problem—that is, the existence of certification programs for jobs that no longer existed—that drove the transformation of the Americanization movement into a precursor to today's adult education programs. Certainly, educators who several years earlier had identified with Americanization programs had begun, by 1927, to identify themselves as "adult educators" rather than as Americanizers.

The distinction was not only semantic. While the explicit project of almost all Americanization courses had been to teach illiterate immigrants "literacy" and "American ways"—however defined—adult educators deliberately created a larger mission for their work. The Department of Immigrant Education itself underwent a name change in 1926 to become the Department of Adult Education, and in its 1927 "Report of the Commission on Coordination in Adult Education" defines its membership as those people who work in "facilities for foreign-born and native-born of all degrees of educational attainment, in schools of elementary, secondary and higher grade, vocational and technical schools, normal schools, colleges, and universities" (Alderman et al. 327). That is, adult education was not limited to immigrants, nor, more important, was the work limited to basic education. Indeed, adult educators were far more likely to emphasize advanced education—particularly at the secondary and tertiary level—than the basic educational initiatives that had been the primary concern of Americanizers.

The results of this shift in definition and emphasis were multiple. At the most basic level, the redefinition succeeded in its underlying aim: to maintain the scholarly and professional positions of teachers who had invested in teacher training for adult courses. More broadly, the move to an adult education model shifted attention to advanced skills and away from the basic skills model embodied most prominently by the Moonlight Schools. In doing so, adult education initiatives participated in the larger cultural shift toward ever more complex literacy skills that Brandt identifies. Chapters 3, 4, and 5 trace the shift from Americanization to adult education and the key role played by the Moonlight Schools in that shift. Chapter 6 examines what this shift can tell us about the history of literacy education as a discipline and our current disciplinary identity.

3. DEVELOPING PEDAGOGIES FOR ILLITERATE ADULTS

𝓔he Moonlight Schools, one of the first organizations that set out to teach a broad scope of reading and writing to adults, began with basic literacy and moved into increasingly complex reading and writing tasks. Many short-term efforts had previously been created to teach specific groups of adults basic literacy—for example, the plantation-based education religious owners provided to their slaves, which focused almost exclusively on reading the Bible (Cornelius), and post–Civil War efforts by Northern reformers and the Freedman's Bureau to educate emancipated slaves. Others had set out to improve the reading and writing skills of the middle classes: both the lyceum movement of the mid-nineteenth century and the job-training correspondence courses of the early twentieth century are examples (Kett; Knowles; Grattan). The Moonlight Schools differed from both of these models in attempting to offer a range of literacy education: the Moonlight Schools were open both to students who were proficient in reading and writing and to those who were without print literacy. Similarly, the schools targeted a wide variety of students: though well-known for their work with rural, white Southerners, Moonlight Schools were organized for urban, middle-class, immigrant, African American, and Native American student populations as well.

The creation of the Moonlight Schools corresponded with an upsurge in public attention to literacy issues. In particular, the influx of non-English-speaking immigrants between 1880 and 1910 inspired vitriolic rhetoric that characterized immigrants as threats to democracy and the American way of life—threats often described in terms of immigrants' perceived illiteracy. In the decade preceding the formation of the Moonlight Schools, Americanization programs were initiated first by business owners and later by civic organizations and public school systems to correct the immigrant "problem" by providing literacy and civic education. Immigrant illiteracy was rhetorically constructed as an educational problem—the immigrants could not write English because they had not been educated (hence, the development of education programs), but, moreover, their presumed refusal to pursue an education was also assumed to reflect a moral deficiency; educating immigrants not only solved the immediate problem of illiteracy but also sought to remedy the moral defects illiteracy "revealed." By conflating "education" and "education in English," this construction denied the fact that many immigrants were literate and educated in their native languages.

Throughout the second and third decades of the twentieth century, efforts to educate "illiterate" adults ("adult" defined here as anyone over eighteen years of age) were under way in two distinct social locations: public night schools and industry-sponsored schools for immigrants and the Moonlight Schools. Though the pedagogical approaches used in both locations have been documented,[1] this scholarship has analyzed each group in isolation, and each has been imagined as responding to a unique set of social conditions. In actual practice, of course, the groups influenced one another, both directly and indirectly. Similarly, both groups responded and reacted to a larger public discussion surrounding student-centered pedagogies inspired by the pedagogical suggestions of John Dewey.

The current chapter places the Moonlight Schools and Americanization classes in relation to one another by examining how each responded to two pedagogical questions: how best to teach students to read and how best to engage students' interest in class material. Then considered is how each group's response to these key pedagogical questions embodies the group's ideological stance toward the role of education in society. By doing so, I suggest that we must come to frame our historical understanding of literacy education in terms of deliberate choices among a variety of possible options that were operating simultaneously. Because the Moonlight Schools have received far less attention than Americanization efforts, the Moonlight Schools' pedagogy is explored in depth in the next section.

Developing Pedagogies for Illiterate Adults

Early Pedagogy and Goals

The first tenet of the Moonlight Schools' pedagogy—and what can be said to be the defining feature of the movement—was that adults should not be imagined (or treated) as analogous to children. Founder Cora Wilson Stewart recognizes that adults' purposes in pursuing education, the kinds of education they require, and the methods through which adults could best learn are significantly different from those of early childhood learners. Importing textbooks and methodology from children's education into adult education initiatives, Stewart suggests, might result in some temporary learning progress among adult students but would ultimately lead to disenchantment with the idea of education. In particular, Stewart believes that adults should not be forced into the "humiliation" of reading material from children's primers (*Moonlight Schools: . . . Illiterates* 23). Instead, Stewart argues that adult primers should feature lessons with two purposes: "the primary one of teaching the pupil to read, and at the same time that of imparting instruction in the things that vitally affected him in his daily life" (71).

The first reader Stewart created for the Moonlight Schools is a simplified newspaper composed of updates on local events. Stewart explains that this text had four benefits:

> To enable adults to learn to read without the humiliation of reading from a child's primer with its lessons on kittens, dolls and toys; to give them a sense of dignity in being, from their very first lessons, readers of a newspaper; to stimulate their curiosity through news of their neighbor's movements and community occurrences and compel them to complete in quick succession the sentences that followed; to arouse them through news of educational and civic improvements in other districts to make like progress in their own. (*Moonlight Schools: . . . Illiterates* 23–24)

As this list of purposes might suggest, Stewart was keenly aware of the need to create a student population for her courses. Indeed, Stewart may be the first major educator to fully engage with the necessity of motivating students to attend classes. For much of US history, school had been perceived as a luxury pursuable only when farm work, local conditions, school resources, and family income would allow: motivation (or lack thereof) was the purview of students and their parents (and, in some areas, clergy). In later years, compulsory attendance motivated students to attend. Though some schools that operated on a profit basis, like the International Correspondence Schools, used advertising as a persuasive means to enroll students, their advertisements are based on the premise that a need was already felt to exist. These advertisements focus primarily on the affordability and convenience of education or the usefulness of particular lessons in obtaining higher pay. The advertisements seem to have adequately addressed their audience; as historian Joseph F. Kett explains, "Most correspondence students seem to have assumed that they already possessed adequate levels of educational attainment and that their principle requirement was the acquisition of job-specific knowledge" (253). Stewart, whose courses were not run for profit and whose target audience had never previously thought of themselves as having access to educational opportunity or had had profoundly unsatisfying experiences with education, had to develop an interest in education among her students if she was to succeed in engaging nonliterate adults in her educational initiative.

Stewart theorizes a number of methods to create interest among her students. This process began with what I am calling a proto-ethnography of literacy. First, Stewart and her teachers set out to "canvass her district in advance to inform the people of the purpose of these schools and to urge them all to attend" (*Moonlight Schools: . . . Illiterates* 15). In the second year of the Moonlight Schools, Stewart completed a fuller "census" that created a

> record, not only the name and age of every illiterate in the county, but his history as well, his ancestry, his home environment, his family ties, his religious faith, his political belief, his weaknesses, tastes and peculiarities, and the influence or combination of influences through which he might be reached in case the teacher failed with him. (*Moonlight Schools: . . . Illiterates* 47)

This information was used to create personalized appeals to residents who had initially refused to become involved with the Moonlight Schools. In one note, a teacher surveying residents points to a courtship as a possible teaching relationship: "Quiet, not talkative, very timid, would be hard to interest. Stays at Mrs. Mauks'. Pays his respects to Mrs. Mauks' daughter. She might teach him" ("Educational Div. No. 1"). Another note suggests that work may be the best motivator: "Sensitive about his illiteracy. Democrat. Born in Ramey Creek, tenants. Just returned from Indiana. Approach him through his employer" ("Educational Div. No. 2"). In her guidebook, Stewart provides an illustrative example of an elderly illiterate woman who had refused all encouragement to attend school. The district teacher, Stewart writes, consulted the "illiteracy record" created by the census, which noted that this woman "thought she was a physician, and felt flattered when anyone sought her services as such" (*Moonlight Schools: . . . Illiterates* 50). Stewart writes that after the teacher visited the woman for medical advice, the woman "concluded that one who possessed such excellent judgment in the selection of a physician, knew enough to teach her something; so while she treated him for erysipelas, he treated her for illiteracy, and she learned to read and write" (*Moonlight Schools: . . . Illiterates* 51). The census gave local teachers the information they needed to make personalized appeals to students, but the proto-ethnographic methods also suggested to students that Moonlight Schools teachers took their students' interests and material conditions seriously. Students were not dismissed or harangued for failure to attend school—instead, teachers sought to meet students on common ground and search for opportunities for mutually beneficial teaching relationships.

Once students made their way to the Moonlight Schools, Stewart focused on creating immediate interest in the purpose of the course. Since students were under no pressure to come to school—and, indeed, material conditions were such that ample pressure existed to prevent students from attending—the Moonlight Schools teachers did not have the luxury of unfolding an elaborate pedagogy that required months or years of student engagement to produce returns: success had to be immediate and compelling. The first lesson of the Moonlight Schools inspired this feeling of success in two ways. First, the text of the first lesson (both in the early newspaper texts and, later, in *The Country Life Readers*, which Stewart also authored) appealed directly to the "ego" of the student (*Moonlight Schools: . . . Illiterates* 71). As Stewart explains, the "essential" elements of the first lesson are "simple words, much repetition and a content that related to the activity of the reader" (21). In keeping with this philosophy, the first lesson of *The Country Life Readers—First Book* reads:

> Can you read?
> Can you write?
> Can you read and write?
> I can read.
> I can write.
> I can read and write.
> Script: I can read and write. (7)[2]

This lesson is designed to instill confidence and pride in the students. The message is one of accomplishment and promise. When students complete the lesson, they make the final line true; they are now able to read and to write. Similarly, the initial questions of the lesson echo questions the students are likely to have encountered; these questions, being asked in the context of a society that values literacy, could have produced feelings of shame, embarrassment, or failure. The lesson gives the students a chance, for the first time in their lives, to answer these questions affirmatively and to feel, in the face of these questions, pride, self-respect, and achievement.

The second method Stewart employed to capture students' interest was teaching students how to write their names in the first class session. As Stewart in *Mother's First Book* instructs, "No other beginning is more inspiring or encouraging"; this lesson represents "a real victory" that "will stimulate [the student] to further progress" (7). To write one's name was to write oneself. The significance of this achievement can be seen even now in present-day research methods used to study the history of literacy; as Harvey Graff explains, "[T]he ability to place a signature [is] the most common historical indicator of the presence of literacy" (14). Beyond its importance as a point of personal pride and literate standing, the ability to write one's name could move students toward more fruitful and secure economic interactions. For instance, Stewart writes of mountaineers who chose not to place their money in banks because they could not sign checks. Those who did choose to participate in social institutions in spite of their illiteracy were at higher risk for a number of economic woes: an X is, after all, much more easily forged than a signature; similarly, the validity of a contract signed with an X could be called into question. Both the Moonlight Schools teachers and their students recognized that the ability to write one's name was the most socially significant lesson that could be taught to illiterate people. Moonlight Schools teachers, working on the rule that sessions ended strictly on time to ensure student safety,[3] did everything possible to make sure that all students left the *first* lesson knowing how to write their own names.

The first lessons appear to have been successful in gaining a student population—certainly, many Moonlight Schools teachers reported encouraging enrollment figures. But the Moonlight Schools, due to the economic and geographic conditions their students faced, had to constantly continue this process of persuasion in order to avoid attrition. The newspaper textbook served to keep students interested in the next news item by featuring local news stories about students' friends and neighbors. These lessons "caused [students] quickly to master the next sentence to see what the next neighbor was doing" (*Moonlight Schools: . . . Illiterates* 24). Stewart also tailored the lessons to appeal to local civic pride and social mores. For instance, one lesson featured the statement that "the best people on earth live in Rowan County," which served to stimulate both interest and a sense of personal and communal pride. News items that celebrated one community—"They are building new steps to the schoolhouse at Slab Camp and putting up hemstitched curtains" (*Moonlight Schools: . . . Illiterates* 24)—inspired others to follow suit and attempt to better the accomplishments so that their doings would likewise be celebrated in this public forum.

Though Stewart's textbooks are focused on teaching basic reading and writing, the Moonlight Schools offered lessons in a variety of other subjects. The list of lessons included "[American] history, civics, English, health and sanitation, geography, home economics, agriculture, horticulture and good roads" (*Moonlight Schools: . . . Illiterates* 26). What made these lessons unique for the time—at least to basic education students—was that they were elective. Students and teachers chose the lessons that would be the focus of each Moonlight Schools session based on which were "the four most suitable to the district's needs" (26). The limited list of available lessons can be read in two ways: it was simply not feasible for Stewart's teachers, who also taught day school, to tailor a wider variety of lessons to their (unpaid) work with adult students, but it was also in keeping with Stewart's motivation for creating the school to limit the lessons to those subjects she felt were necessary to lift the people out of their "stagnation." However interpreted, the variability of the Moonlight Schools' lessons was pedagogically and theoretically innovative: the underlying philosophy of this choice posits that uneducated students are capable of directing their own education.

As these early lessons indicate, the Moonlight Schools' pedagogy was political in the sense that Stewart and her fellow teachers set out to inculcate their students with middle-class values "through suggestion, if through nothing else" (*Moonlight Schools:... Illiterates* 72).[4] The repetition of words and phrases in each lesson was designed to help students practice reading and writing words, but a useful by-product of this necessary repetition was to expose students to "good thoughts" and "good words." As Stewart explains, "The copying of the script sentences in the book pledged the students to progress and impressed upon him certain evils with fine psychological effect" (72). The principles expressed in these repeated phrases are, without exception, statements that reflect a bourgeois understanding of "good": good roads, good hygiene, paying taxes, keeping a painted house, and putting money in the bank, for example. Lessons on values that reflected a lower-class background—but which were deeply held in the area—are absent from all of Stewart's texts: there are no lessons, for instance, on maintaining family bonds (a potential source for violent feuds), hunting, or foraging,[5] though these practices were often more likely to represent the values and experiences of Moonlight Schools students than lessons emphasizing good roads and banking.

Baldwin suggests that Stewart's appeal to middle-class values may have been inspired by Stewart's childhood experiences during the Rowan County War, a feud between the Martin and Tolliver families that was "the bloodiest feud in the state's history [surpassing] even the Hatfield-McCoy vendetta in numbers of dead" (15). Because she grew up during the war and saw its effects directly as wounded men visited her father's medical office, Stewart was particularly invested in changing those social features that were (she believed) responsible for promulgating feud culture. As such, Stewart made clear that part of her mission in bringing literacy to Rowan County and the mountains more generally was to put an end to the social and economic conditions that spawned such bloodshed.

In her quest to improve mountain life, Stewart in many ways embraced what Graff has termed the literacy myth, which holds that "primary schooling and literacy are necessary ... for economic and social development, establishment and maintenance of democratic institutions, individual advancement, and so on" (xxxviii). Much of the rhetoric surrounding the

Moonlight Schools movement—especially public speeches designed for fund-raising—reflects the linkage between literacy and social and economic advancement that is a cornerstone of the literacy myth. For instance, Stewart often represents illiteracy as a form of "slavery" from which the Moonlight Schools can "emancipate" students. Similarly, Stewart's suggestion that teaching literacy was a deterrent to crime echoes the literacy myth's claim that literacy brought both social and economic benefits to individuals and communities.

Though Stewart does impute a great deal to literacy learning, the Moonlight Schools' underlying philosophy indicates a more nuanced view of the benefits of literacy than is evident in the literacy myth. Stewart's decision to include lessons on banking, hygiene, politics, agriculture, and infrastructure suggests that she was aware that literacy alone would not be enough to improve her students' lives. Certainly, Stewart was under no obligation to address these issues, since her local news readers were so successful that these could well have served as the only text for the course. Her decision to include lessons on "good thoughts" and social and economic issues speaks to her belief that these were key elements in uplifting her students. Literacy was but one among many knowledges that the Moonlight Schools sought to provide, and though Stewart considered literacy essential to social advancement, she also saw a basic knowledge of history, math, and hygiene, in particular, as equally important.

More important, Stewart makes no attempt to suggest that social mobility and economic mobility are the exclusive purview of literate people. She writes, for instance, of men who celebrate that they will no longer have to sign by mark at the bank, indicating that these men were *already* bank patrons. In *Moonlight Schools: For the Emancipation of Adult Illiterates*, Stewart also includes a number of stories of men and women who held highly respected positions but who were illiterate or poorly educated: school board members, preachers, and postmasters, for instance, were among the first Moonlight Schools students. The text is filled with stories of community leaders who "had seized this opportunity to break up the stagnation which had overtaken them" (42): teachers, doctors, merchants, and mill owners. Stewart celebrates as an ideal the two school trustees who, after attending a Moonlight School, were "so delighted with [their] progress that [they] enrolled, also, in the day school" (39). Though the Moonlight Schools explicitly aimed to improve students' social and economic conditions, the schools suggested that intellectual mobility—the ability to change one's way of thinking—was the most important key to and marker of success.

The key to intellectual mobility, the Moonlight Schools' curriculum suggested, was not any isolated skill or individual achievement but rather a communal desire to learn together. At a basic level, Stewart had to promote the idea that rural communities *could* live in harmony, that individuals could peacefully coexist with one another, before any further steps could be taken toward improving students' lives. Literacy meant little in a war zone. In response to this need for harmony, Stewart frames her students as coming "in quest of knowledge" (*Moonlight Schools: . . . Illiterates* 42) and finding in the schools both knowledge and a sense of community. The Moonlight Schools led to a variety of social improvements; one man claims that after three weeks of at a Moonlight School,

> we papered the [school]house, put in new windows, purchased new stovepipe, made new steps, contributed money, and bought the winter's fuel. Now we have a live Sunday school, a singing school, prayer meeting once each week, and preaching twice a month. . . . Good roads clubs, fruit clubs, agricultural clubs, home economics clubs, and Sunday schools were organized. (45)

Stewart suggests that this newfound social drive for "improvement" is derived not from any direct connection to literacy but from the experience of learning: "Men and women who had hitherto been divided by contention and strife now worked side by side in concord. They were schoolmates and that is a tie that binds" (46).

To build these ties further, the Moonlight Schools encouraged students to become teachers. Adults who had attended the first two sessions of the Moonlight Schools were enlisted to carry out the third year's mission: the elimination of illiteracy in Rowan County. As Stewart explains, men and women who had learned to read and write in previous sessions "became at once a source of pride and admiration to [their] neighbors, as well as to [themselves] and family, and, like most new converts to a cause, [they] exceeded the old adherents in loyalty and zeal" (*Moonlight Schools: . . . Illiterates* 48). The Moonlight Schools corps of day school teachers encouraged students to become "successful teachers" themselves; the students "attempted to give lessons in reading and writing only and to create that self-confidence, which, with adult illiterates, was the first battle to be won" (49). Always in search of new ways to engage potential students, Stewart points out that these newly educated students had a key advantage over the trained teachers: "they had the advantage . . . of presenting themselves as examples, as living proof that illiterates could learn" (49).

Though illiteracy is the focal point of this communal effort, the measure of success Stewart employs is not solely the number of people taught (or not taught) but also the community-building results of the project. The slogan adopted for the Moonlight Schools' outreach program was, "Each one teach one," and by Stewart's account, this message was taken literally:

> Doctors were soon teaching their convalescent patients, ministers were teaching members of their flocks, children were teaching their parents, stenographers were teaching waitresses in the small town hotels, and the person in the county without a pupil was considered a very useless sort of individual. (*Moonlight Schools: . . . Illiterates* 48)

When Stewart describes one community celebrating the completion of its illiteracy drive, she emphasizes not just the reading and writing ability on display—the students not only "read and wrote," they "quoted history and ciphered proudly" (52)—but also the feeling of community among all involved. She explains that "every person in the district was at the school-house" for the graduation, with a "cordon of spectators six rows deep" (53). More important, the community meeting reflects the change in attitudes that is the core goal of the Moonlight Schools; one old man relates, "Things have certainly changed in this district. It used to be that you couldn't hold meeting or Sunday school in this house without the boys shooting through the windows. It used to be moonshine and bullets; but now it's lemonade and Bibles" (53).[6] Other Moonlight Schools teachers reported similar results. R. E. Jaggers, for instance, reported that "community spirit was aroused almost universally wherever a school was taught because it was the means of bringing all factions together on a common ground and forced them to act together" (qtd. in Kentucky Illiteracy Commission 6).[7] Moonlight Schools supporters suggested that the very experience of working together in the school building made other forms of community participation viable in previously feud-ravaged communities.

Phonics versus Whole-Word Pedagogies

To create pedagogies that would both engage and educate adults, Stewart and her fellow Moonlight Schools teachers selected from among existing pedagogical methods designed for children and adapted these pedagogies to suit the needs of adults. The state of educational research left Moonlight Schools teachers with few other options; as the International Reading Association, Jill Fitzgerald, and H. Alan Robinson explain,

> [N]ineteenth century author-educators . . . [made] no clear distinction between the reading processes of the child or "little adult" and the mature adult reader. They believed that both children and adults went through similar steps in order to read and while reading. What distinguished the child from the adult was simply age and experience and the difficulty level of the materials used. (10)

Stewart, however, believed that adults and children were fundamentally different: different in their interests, their experiences, and their needs. Pedagogies had to respond to these differences or risk infantilizing—and driving away—adult students. Because no adult-oriented pedagogies yet existed, the Moonlight Schools teachers drew from child education research, employing those elements that seemed useful and discarding those that might impede or insult adult learners.

The first and perhaps most important pedagogical choice facing Stewart and her teachers was what method of reading instruction to employ in the schools. In 1911, two distinct varieties of reading education existed: phonics-based instruction and whole-word instruction. Of the two, phonics instruction had a much-longer history: the International Reading Association, Fitzgerald, and Robinson, as well as Miriam Balmuth, date the use of phonics in US reading instruction to at least as early as 1793. Early American phonics instruction heavily emphasized spelling as well as proper oral delivery of written material; all lessons were intended to be read aloud by students. As Nila Banton Smith explains, Noah Webster's immensely popular reader *The American Spelling Book* (1790) began its lessons with "the alphabet, syllables, and consonant combinations. The second page for a child to read contained 197 syllables. The succeeding several pages were devoted to lists of words arranged in order by their numbers of syllables" (42).

By the mid-nineteenth century, phonics pedagogies were often blended with "alphabetic" methods to produce systems that "reduced the number of characters needed in representing the sounds in the English language by respelling words and by omitting silent letters" (N. Smith 120). In this model, spelling was deemphasized in favor of easier pronunciation. This shift in phonics instruction was a response to a new pedagogical approach to reading: the whole-word method. As explained by an early advocate, Samuel Worcester, whole-word pedagogies were based on the premise that children "may first learn to read words by seeing them, hearing them pronounced, and having their meanings illustrated, and afterward [the child] may learn to analyze them or name the letters of which they are composed" (qtd. in N. Smith 81). Whole-word pedagogies began with "familiar and easy *words*, instead of *letters*" (Josiah Bumstead, qtd. in N. Smith 81). Though the earliest examples of whole-word pedagogies reverted to phonics methods after the child's initial immersion in reading, later iterations provided very little phonics or spelling instruction.

Though historians of literacy education identify a variety of origins for whole-word pedagogies, many, including Geraldine Rodgers, Balmuth, and Nila Smith, argue that Horace Mann was largely responsible for popularizing whole-word approaches among American educators. Mann initially advocated whole-word pedagogies because he believed in the "need to arouse the desire to learn"—and the immediate success offered by reading entire words was, he believed, a more compelling motivation for students than phonics learning (Balmuth 190). In his later career, Mann became an increasingly fervent advocate of whole-word pedagogies; he described alphabetic lists as "skeleton-shaped, bloodless, ghostly apparitions, and hence it is no wonder that children look and feel so deathlike, when compelled to face them" ("Lecture," part 2, 27) whereas whole-word lessons would "be like an excursion to the fields of elysium, compared with the old method" ("Lecture," part 3, 47). Echoing Mann's own progression into a whole-word apostle, whole-word pedagogies were initially imagined as a supplement to phonics approaches, but they quickly became the dominant method of reading instruction in the United States; many educators rejected phonics entirely.

Anecdotal evidence from the nineteenth century—there were no scientific studies of reading conducted prior to 1910 (Balmuth; Rodgers; N. Smith)—suggests that whole-word approaches gained popularity for precisely the reason Mann identified: they did succeed in engaging children in the reading process.[8] However, many educators also discovered that "children who had been taught by this method were not able to read well in the upper grades" (N. Smith 124). As a result, the phonics method began to regain popularity in the last decade of the nineteenth century. As Rebecca Pollard, a prominent nineteenth-century phonics advocate, explains, "By [the whole-word] method the word is presented to the child as a whole, and the teacher either tells the child the word, or by skillful questioning leads him to use the word. . . . He [the student] soon learns to think he can do nothing with a new word without the help of the teacher in some way" (203). Instead, Pollard asks, "[I]s it not infinitely better to take the sounds of the letters for our starting point, and with these sounds lay a foundation . . . upon which we can build whole families of words for instant recognition?" (3). By 1911, the year Stewart began the Moonlight Schools, phonics instruction had (re)gained many supporters, and a wide variety of children's primers existed for both phonics and whole-word methods.

Because at least half of every Moonlight Schools session was devoted to reading and writing[9] and because the schools sought to eliminate illiteracy, the choice of reading pedagogy was the key to the Moonlight Schools' success (or failure). As argued above, the first challenge facing the Moonlight Schools was to create and maintain a student population. Stewart, then, opted to employ a whole-word pedagogy in all Moonlight Schools texts and primers because whole-word pedagogies were recognized by nearly all reading advocates as more immediately interesting to students. As she explains in her yearly pedagogical bulletins, issued by the Kentucky Illiteracy Commission, "The lessons in the *Country Life Readers* are adapted to the words and sentence method. Whole sentences are first taught, and later a drill on words may be given" (*Moonlight Schools . . . Reconstruction* 13). Stewart also emphasizes that "spelling is not employed in the beginning, lest it hamper reading, and confuse the pupils. After they have lessons in reading, and know a number of sentences and words[,] they can begin to spell. Written spelling may form some of their writing exercises after they have learned to write" (*Moonlight Schools . . . Reconstruction* 14).

Stewart gives a more in-depth description of her pedagogy in the last primer she composed, *Mother's First Book*. In her "Instructions to Teacher" section, she describes the reading process:

The first reading lesson should be made interesting by conversation, in which the pupil is led by the teacher's questions and suggestions to speak the sentence before she sees it in print. Then when it is presented, the teacher may say, "Here are the words in print that you have just spoken—'See my baby.'" . . . At first, she should read it under the teacher's guidance, taking the teacher's word for it that it reads—"See my baby." Later, after each sentence has been read in this manner . . . she should be drilled on recognizing and naming the words until she knows each of them by sight. Then the actual reading begins. She should read each sentence through without assistance, recognizing each of the words. By this plan, first the sentence as a whole, then the words composing it, are taught. This plan should be followed throughout the succeeding lessons. (8–9)

Notably, Stewart's description of her pedagogy echoes precisely the pedagogy that Pollard had critiqued twenty years earlier as failing to prepare students for reading new material outside the teacher's immediate presence. Given the widespread discussion of phonics and whole-word approaches in educational journals and textbooks, Stewart would have been aware of the critiques of whole-word pedagogies. Her decision to embrace whole-word methods, then, should be read as a deliberate choice among two equally viable and, therefore, as reflective of her teaching philosophy.

Stewart's choice, as her remarks throughout *Moonlight Schools* make clear, hinged on motivation: adult students had to experience immediate success if they were to continue with the educational program. As Mann had suggested almost a century prior, whole-word approaches were recognized, even among phonics advocates, as highly successful in gaining student interest and in teaching basic reading skills. Also, because phonics pedagogies were associated with children's reading in a way that word reading was not—all readers read words, but only beginning readers underwent phonics drills—using phonics with adults could have produced feelings of resentment or shame. Conversely, reading words connoted advanced reading: previously illiterate adults could now perform the same reading act—the act of reading a sentence—as long-time readers. Finally, whole-word approaches allowed Stewart to avoid the difficulties of implementing a phonics-based pedagogy in a region where students and teachers spoke different dialects. Because some phonemes of the Appalachian dialect spoken among mountaineers were distinct from the Bluegrass dialect spoken by Stewart and many of her teachers, either teachers or students would have had to adapt to a new phonetic system for the teaching to succeed.[10]

Stewart's choice of whole-word pedagogies reflects her long-term goals for her students. Stewart was extremely explicit about her primary goals, both in her textbooks and in other forums: to teach students to write only as well as necessary to allow them to communicate their thoughts. In *Mother's First Book*, for instance, Stewart reminds teachers that they must "keep before the pupil this objective: the writing of her first letter" (8). In her specific calls for funding and volunteers, Stewart set forth numbers of students to be made literate: in her 1917 "A Call to the Teachers," for instance, Stewart asks, "SHALL KENTUCKY SEND THIRTY THOUSAND ILLITERATES TO FRANCE? God forbid! Why should she send any? Hasn't she an Illiteracy Commission, 11,000 public school teachers and as patriotic people as ever the sun shone on?"[11] Stewart most succinctly states her purpose in her private correspondence; in a letter to close friend A. E. Winship, she explains, "We have a very definite proposition—it is simply to teach five million people to write and to do it in a given time" (Stewart, Letter to A. E. Winship).

Stewart explains in *Moonlight Schools* that the schools' elective drills "attempted nothing more ambitious in the beginning sessions than to clear up such wrong impressions" as "Uncle Sam, our President of the United States, is a grand old man" (*Moonlight Schools: . . . Illiterates* 25). Similarly, her lessons in reading and writing attempted nothing more ambitious than to prepare students for simple textual interactions. Even in the *Country Life Readers—Second Book*, the most difficult texts students were expected to read are drawn from the Bible. While the Bible is, of course, a complex text, students would not be reading this text without guidance; they received such guidance every Sunday and often on Wednesdays, too. The texts Stewart composed prepare students to write letters to friends and family and to read letters in return—letters that require little formal expertise, for friends and family are unlikely to judge harshly. Other than the Bible, the local newspaper is the most difficult text that students are expected to read. While *The Indian's First Book* does attempt to prepare students for more formal interactions with government agents, these interactions are designed to express the students' needs in as few words as possible, and students are provided with templates for future use.

Because Stewart aimed at comparatively basic skills, the primary drawback of whole-word pedagogies—students' inability to read complex texts in higher grades—was negated. While Stewart certainly hoped that some students would go on to higher educational achievement (see Stewart, Letter to A. E. Winship), she recognized that few would or could pursue this course. Since students were unlikely to benefit from the long-term advantages of phonics pedagogies, the benefits of whole-word pedagogies—the immediate sense of success provided by reading words, and the difference between whole-word and the phonics pedagogies associated with childhood learning—far outweighed the potential drawbacks.

Adapting Educational Discourse to Local Communities' Needs

That Stewart valued her students' abilities and experience and that her educational purpose was to prepare students to participate in their local communities are also evident in her commitment to an experience-based model of education. Though archival evidence does not exist to confirm direct influences on Moonlight Schools' pedagogies, the schools' appeal to locally relevant pedagogies closely mirrored the child-centered, experiential pedagogies John Dewey and his many proponents developed. As with her decision to embrace whole-word pedagogies, Stewart's decision to employ a Deweyan model of experiential pedagogies represents a deliberate choice among many existing pedagogical theories and should be read as evidence of the school's philosophical underpinnings.

Much of Dewey's most respected work postdates the foundation of the Moonlight Schools.[12] However, Dewey had published several works outlining his pedagogical principles prior to 1911 and was already recognized as a leading educational theorist.[13] In *My Pedagogic Creed*, Dewey emphasizes the importance of addressing students' life experiences; he asserts that "the school must represent present life—life as real and vital to the child as that which he carries on in the home, in the neighborhood, or on the play-ground" and that "the school life should grow gradually out of the home life; that it should take up and continue the activities with which the child is already familiar in the home" (7–8). In his later work *The Child and the Curriculum*, Dewey suggests that if the school does not reflect the child's experience, three "evils" result:

In the first place, a lack of any organic connection with what the child has already seen and felt and loved makes the material purely formal and symbolic. . . . A symbol which is induced without, which has not been led up to in previous activities is, as we say, a *bare* or *mere* symbol. . . . The second evil . . . is lack of motivation. . . . The third evil is that even the most scientific matter, arranged in most logical fashion, loses this quality, when presented in external, ready-made fashion, by the time it gets to the child. . . . Those things which are most valuable to the scientific man, and the most valuable in the logic of actual inquiry and classification, drop out. (31–33)

Dewey posits that by creating lessons that draw from students' previous experiences, teachers could illustrate relationships between students' lives and class material, which give students a reason to engage with unfamiliar topics and help students grasp increasingly complex concepts.

Dewey also argues that education should itself take place through experiences. Action, he states, is the central source of consciousness and, thus, of learning;

I believe the active side precedes the passive in the development of the child nature; that expression comes before conscious impression; that the muscular development precedes the sensory; that movements come before conscious sensations; I believe that consciousness is essentially motor or impulsive; that conscious states tend to project themselves in action. (*My Pedagogic* 13)

In short, students learn first and best by *doing* activities, not by listening to lectures. Actions, Dewey believes, are the center of social life; the purpose of education is "to enable [the child] to perform those fundamental types of activity which makes civilization what it is" (11). In light of the importance of actions, Dewey argues that "cooking, sewing, manual training, etc." should be central elements of the curriculum:

I believe that they are not special studies which are to be introduced over and above a lot of others in the way of relaxation or relief, or as additional accomplishments. I believe rather that they represent, as types, fundamental forms of social activity; and that it is possible and desirable that the child's introduction into the more formal subjects of the curriculum be through the medium of these activities. (11)

Forcing students to sit passively and "absorb" lessons, Dewey believes, accomplished remarkably little: by encouraging students to learn through action, teachers are embracing children's natural tendencies toward movement and preparing them to participate in their society.

The Moonlight Schools' pedagogical philosophy closely resembles the experience-based model Dewey had popularized throughout the previous decade. In fact, Stewart argues that making connections between the students' everyday lives and the content of lessons "in adult education is even more necessary than in that of the child" (*Moonlight Schools: . . . Illiterates* 71). As the Moonlight Schools expanded beyond Rowan County, the production of specially designed newspapers became impracticable, yet there were no existing primers that addressed adults' daily lives. To meet the need, Stewart wrote primers to be used in the schools. The first of these, *The Country Life Readers*, was designed to respond to the daily lives and experiences of rural people. The *Country Life Readers, First Book*, includes lessons on wagon upkeep, pesticide use, corn planting, crop rotation, and forest management. The text also includes lessons aimed at homemakers: lessons on the benefits of fresh air for children, ways to cook corn, potatoes, and meat, and methods for creating a yeast colony are included, intermixed with farming and civics lessons. Stewart also takes the opportunity to advocate for better conditions for women: one lesson points out that a woman carries "more than two thousand" buckets of water a year from the well to the house. Students are asked to read and write, "I will pipe water into my house and save my wife" (56).

The early lessons in the *First Book* are so short and simple that students are unlikely to glean new information: most farmers would already know, for instance, that a silo's purpose is to keep fodder moist. But this is the point: students are already familiar with the concepts and experiences described, and this familiarity helps students decode the text and process the new skills involved in reading. In later lessons, after students master the basic principles of word recognition, the *First Book* begins to introduce content lessons as well. Drawing from existing lesson structures used frequently in children's primers, Stewart employs two varieties of lessons to persuade students to adopt new methods even as they increase their literacy abilities. In the first of these structures, Stewart describes a positive farming experience. For instance,

Developing Pedagogies for Illiterate Adults

Farmer Brown raises good fruit.
Do you know how he does it?
I will tell you.
He sprays all his fruit trees.
He takes good care of them.
That is why he has fine fruit.
It sells at a good price.
It pays Farmer Brown to spray his fruit trees. (20)

Stewart then juxtaposes this positive image with a negative version in the following lesson:

Farmer Jones does not raise good fruit.
Do you know why?
He does not spray his fruit trees.
He has very poor fruit. (21)

By maintaining similar sentence structures in each lesson, Stewart improved students' chances of reading success. Since the Moonlight Schools emphasized sight reading, seeing the same words used in slightly different contexts helped increase students' vocabulary while maintaining confidence: after learning the Farmer Brown lesson, students would be able to read over half of the words in the following lesson, and the similarity of the sentence structure helps students to infer the meaning of those words not featured in the previous story. But the lessons also provide a rationale for what was, as yet, an uncommon practice in many rural areas: the use of pesticides. The question that ends the Farmer Jones lesson—"Shall I be foolish like Farmer Jones or wise like Farmer Brown?"—frames students as perpetuating their ignorance if they continue to forgo spraying. Given that the lesson is provided in a school, by a book, and in the presence of a teacher charged with providing instruction to these farmers, the lesson's admonition carries a great deal of cultural weight; Stewart could have done little more to ensure the adoption of progressive farming methods, methods she suggested could alleviate the poverty and ill health that plagued rural people.

The second lesson structure emphasizes student experience through an informational dialogue. In these conversations, one speaker functions as a stand-in for the students; the other offers useful advice. Though the adviser is positioned as more knowledgeable, the conversation is framed as occurring between equals: the adviser functions to augment, rather than contradict, the students' existing knowledge. In one lesson, two women have a conversation about creating a yeast colony:

> "How good the bread looks! How often do you make it?"
> "I make it every week; don't you?"
> "No, I never make light bread. I have no yeast. You cannot make light bread without yeast."
> "I am going to make some yeast cakes and I will give you some. Then you can always have yeast.
> "I will tell you how I make it." (*Country Life Readers—First* 60–61)

The lesson then gives a description of how to produce a yeast colony with potatoes and sugar. Here, the student is framed as holding some knowledge: that light bread cannot be made without yeast. Though the adviser knows more than the student, both are working from a set of shared knowledges. The student's existing knowledge of bread and cooking processes sets the terms through which the new content knowledge—yeast production—is introduced.

In combination with these experience-based reading lessons, Stewart also incorporates Deweyan concepts of experiential learning by augmenting the course texts with specific activities. The *First Book's* "Suggestions to Teachers" section offers that "for teaching the banking lesson . . . a supply of blank checks should be provided in advance. . . . Then, after a line is read in concert, the action mentioned should be performed by the class" (4). To accompany the lesson on spraying pesticides, Stewart encourages teachers to exhibit examples of treated and untreated fruits. And after a lesson on voting, "A temporary voting booth can be arranged, election officers appointed, and blank ballots, previously prepared, should be voted" (5). Stewart, like Dewey, argues that these experiential lessons "both give an added interest to the subject and impress the principles of the same" (4).

As the Moonlight Schools became a national movement, the student demographic broadened; lessons on rural life did not adequately respond to the life experiences of all students. Also, because the schools aimed to teach students progressive farming, cooking, and sanitation methods, as well as to improve students' knowledge of history and world events, the readers were not sufficient to keep teachers and students up-to-date with new developments. To address these problems, Stewart used Kentucky Illiteracy Commission funds to produce a course book for each year of the commission's existence, and she later published textbooks that targeted specific student populations: soldiers, American Indians, and mothers.[14]

The first of these targeted textbooks, *The Soldier's First Book*, was designed to be used in army camps before soldiers deployed overseas. Because soldiers were drafted from all regions of the country and from a variety of professions, students shared little preexisting common experience from which Stewart could draw lessons. Instead, *The Soldier's First Book* includes lessons on camp life, an experience that all students shared but one that was new and unfamiliar to most. *The Soldier's First Book* served as both a reading primer and a primer on proper behavior for new soldiers, presenting men with basic information essential to camp life yet so fundamental that few officers recognized the need to explain the concept to inexperienced draftees.

Many of the lessons in the textbook are designed to prevent embarrassment. For instance, Stewart describes a common prank played on new recruits:

> Let us play a joke on a rookie.
> All right. What shall it be?
> Send him after a key.
> A key to what?
> A key to the parade ground.
> Is that a joke?
> Can you not see it?
> No, I cannot.
> Did you ever see a key to a field?
> No. I see. The joke is on me. (*Soldier's First Book*, lesson 8)

As in *Country Life Readers*, the structure of the lesson allows for a high degree of repetition, reinforcing word recognition, and ensuring that students will be able to decode many of the words on the page, increasing self-esteem. But the passage also provides a content lesson: recruits are not only warned about the specific prank described but are also made aware that pranks are a part of army life. Moreover, these lessons were particularly pertinent for illiterate, rural soldiers because they were likely to be targeted for these kinds of pranks. The lesson also demonstrates one structure used

Developing Pedagogies for Illiterate Adults

for pranks: in theory, students could use this information to more fully participate in camp life by pulling their own pranks.

The Soldier's First Book also provides lessons in terminology. One lesson defines "rookie"; another defines "A.W.O.L." Yet another offers a series of important definitions not provided in standard army manuals but which functioned as an assumed common knowledge among experienced soldiers:

> Let's go to the canteen.
> The canteen! Where is it?
> It is over there to the right.
> What is the canteen?
> Why, rookie, don't you know?
> No, if I did, I wouldn't ask.
> It is where they keep the "dope and smokes."
> "Dope and smokes." What are they?
> Soft drinks and cigars.
> I'll take water, thank you, and a good book. (Lesson 13)

Though Stewart's final line is perhaps more idealistic than practical, the remainder of the lesson provides a useful guide to army jargon. The speaker, who functions as a stand-in for all rookie soldiers, asks the somewhat embarrassing questions—What is the canteen? What are "dope and smokes"?—so that the soldiers themselves do not have acknowledge their own inexperience.

The later lessons in *The Soldier's First Book* forgo basic army knowledge in favor of inspirational texts: through a selection of poems and stories about patriotic figures, the text ties soldier students' activities to a history of valor and courage. Though these lessons are certainly idealistic—almost trite—they nevertheless appeal to students' self-esteem and work to build a sense of common experience: previous soldiers, the lessons suggest, have undergone similar trials. Like the terminology lessons, the patriotic lessons employ student experience as a tool to motivate students to engage with the text: because the reading materials were immediately relevant to their lives, students were more likely to continue with the educational program and to understand increasingly complex reading texts.

The Soldier's First Book was well received; the YMCA ordered thousands of copies for use in army camps, and Stewart received letters from military students just as she had from earlier Moonlight Schools students testifying that they had learned to read and write through the lessons. This success affirmed Stewart's belief in the need to tailor instruction to particular student populations, and she produced two additional textbooks in the following decade: *The Indian's First Book* and *Mother's First Book*. Though *The Indian's First Book* was not issued in bound form, mimeographed versions of the text were employed in all reservation Moonlight Schools for which Stewart kept records.

In *The Indian's First Book*, Stewart faced a challenge: her educational philosophy demanded that she connect the readings to students' daily lives, but the Moonlight Schools courses held on reservations were sponsored by the Bureau of Indian Affairs, an organization that aimed to *change* the daily lives of Native Americans. If Stewart embraced Native American traditions, students would be more likely to engage with the text, but the bureau would be unlikely to print it. If Stewart promoted middle-class values, as she had in the *Country Life Readers*, Native American students might refuse to read the text, seeing it as yet another colonizing force the government introduced.

Likely in response to this dilemma, *The Indian's First Book* avoids the conversational lessons that dominate the *Country Life Readers* in favor of first-person narratives. By employing first person, the text itself frames Native Americans as authorities on their own lives: an outside adviser does not attempt to teach the Native American speaker how to better himself. Furthermore, these first-person narratives are framed in terms of economic success and family life; there are no lessons, such as those in the *Country Life Readers*, that emphasize social standing or cultural capital.

Stewart also balances images of the sedentary farming life, sponsored by the Bureau of Indian Affairs, with discussion of existing practices. Because most of the reservation courses were conducted in Montana, North Dakota, South Dakota, and the Far West, Stewart included lessons on hunting and fishing as well as gardening and raising livestock. One lesson, for instance, celebrates hunting skill:

> This is the deer I hunted.
> It is a big deer.
> I shot it in the mountains.
> Do you like to hunt deer?
> I like to hunt deer in the mountains.
> The deer runs fast.
> I like to chase him. (Lesson 7)

By including these lessons early in the text, Stewart establishes credibility for the book. While the first lessons are essentially identical to those in the *Country Life Readers* and sought to inspire immediate confidence, the next group of lessons demonstrates to students that the text is not—or is not only—an attempt to denigrate their experiences and ways of life. Instead, the text recognizes that the daily activities of many Native American men (and women) include more variety than the Bureau of Indian Affairs might wish.[15]

Despite these early connections to existing practices, much of the text does embrace the model of sedentary farming the Bureau of Indian Affairs encouraged. But rather than present this lifestyle as innately "better" than students' traditions, Stewart emphasizes instead the economic benefits of participating in farming. For instance,

> I have some sheep.
> My sheep have good wool and fat lambs.
> I can sell my lambs and wool.
> Indians make fine blankets from wool.
> My sheep will make me much money.
> Sheep do not eat so much as cattle.
> I will raise more sheep. (Lesson 16)

Another lesson describes children joining an agricultural club and asserts, "Pigs and poultry will bring them money" (Lesson 24). Similarly, writing is framed as a way to intercede with the government to obtain more money. A sample letter to a BIA agent reads:

> My little boy is going to school. He needs money to buy books and clothing. Please send ten dollars quick. I do not want my boy to miss school. I want him to learn to read and write. So please send his money. (Lesson 23)

Nearly all lessons share this economic emphasis. The few lessons that stray from the economic focus emphasize health and well-being, particularly the need for children to drink milk and eat a variety of foods. In both cases, the lessons describe concrete actions and concrete benefits.

By emphasizing monetary benefits, Stewart balances the need to motivate Native Americans to read with the need to appease the Bureau of Indian Affairs. Though many lessons endorse the lifestyle the bureau encouraged, this endorsement is framed solely in economic terms. The lessons appeal to material conditions rather than moral or civic platitudes: though farming on the reservations may not be ideal, fair, or desirable, it is nevertheless the only available option for most Native Americans, particularly those enrolled in bureau Moonlight Schools. The lessons in the primer emphasize, as do Stewart's earlier drills, the behaviors needed to "get by" in the students' social milieu, and they appeal to students by speaking to the realities of their experience. Perhaps more important, Stewart also appeals to students by refusing to employ the civic and moralistic appeals common to government rhetoric, thus distancing the textbook, to some extent, from the government agency that distributed it.

Mother's First Book seems to have presented a similar rhetorical quandary for Stewart. As explained in chapter 4, Stewart strongly disagreed with members of the Americanization movement. Stewart believed that Americanizers failed to recognize that many immigrants were educated and literate in their native languages, and she disapproved of the link Americanizers suggested between literacy and American identity. However, Americanization courses were by far the largest site of adult education in the United States, and Americanizers were well funded: these educators could afford to purchase and distribute Stewart's textbooks, while many Moonlight Schools teachers could not. By selling *Mother's First Book* to Americanizers, Stewart could produce income to feed back into her Moonlight Schools work.[16] But *Mother's First Book* also needed to respond to the needs of rural mothers: while the *Country Life Readers* include some lessons on homemaking subjects, the text is, at heart, a reader for male farmers. Moreover, the *Country Life Readers* were designed for classroom use, and their experiential lesson plans were designed for groups. But many mothers were unable to attend regular evening sessions because of their childcare responsibilities. *Mother's First Book* was "designed for use in the home," for individual women being taught "by the public school teacher or by an ex-teacher; or, if not by these, by a member of the woman's own family, by a neighbor or friend" (5). Two competing aims framed the work of the book: to appeal to immigrant educators' efforts to reform "foreign" practices and to appeal to rural women's experiences to maximize their engagement with the text.

To meet these competing aims, Stewart focuses on universal homemaking activities that would be common for both immigrant and rural women. Many lessons discuss basic childcare; for instance, the third lesson reads:

What can I do for the baby?
I can keep the baby warm.
I can keep the baby clean.
I can keep the baby quiet.
I can keep the baby well fed. (13)

Nearly all the lessons in *Mother's First Book* appeal to middle-class mores, emphasizing the "virtues" of cleanliness, hard work, and thrift. While these are but three of many of the values associated with the middle class, these three are particularly appropriate for *Mother's First Book* because they respond to prevalent stereotypes of both rural and immigrant women as unclean, lazy, and lax with money.[17] To emphasize these values "through suggestion, if through nothing else" (*Moonlight Schools: . . . Illiterates* 72) and to speak directly to the immediate experience of students—students who are sitting *in their homes* as the lessons are read—Stewart provides readings on basic home upkeep that explicitly characterize "better" and "nice" homes and people as "clean" and "neat":

Here is a real home!
See how neat and clean it is.
. . .
My family can work here.
My family can be happy here.
I will keep my home neat and clean. (18)

In another passage, women are asked to read the lines "I have a nice, clean family. They shall have nice, clean clothes" (24), and the readers are taught that the "best way" to wash dishes is to "prepare well and take pride in the job" (39). Other lessons extol the benefits of work:

Day is the time for work.
I am glad to work.
Work is good for me. (21)

and encourage students to save the money they make: "I can have a brand new five-dollar bill, and when I get it I will save it, too" (32).

Stewart makes no secret of her desire to see women adopt the practices she describes in these lessons. In the book's introduction, she explains that the lessons "aim not only at teaching women to read and write, but at leading them to better home practices and higher ideals in their home and community life" (6). While Stewart aims at much the same goals in the *Country Life Readers*, the structures of the lessons in *Mother's First Book* are quite different. There are no juxtapositions of positive and negative examples, and while dialogue lessons are still used frequently, these dialogues are evenly divided: in some, an adviser provides useful information to an interested, capable woman (who functions as a stand-in for the reader); in others, the *reader* is positioned as the informed party within the dialogue, dispensing knowledge to a less-educated friend. For instance, women read:

> A woman asked me, "Why is it that your family is seldom sick? Why do they look so strong, and keep so well?"
>
> "I keep them clean, I see that they have fresh air, and exercise, I see that they have plenty of sleep, and I feed them the right sort of food," I told her. (50–51)

In other cases, the lesson structures are similar to those used in *The Indian's First Book*: the lessons are written in first person and extol the abilities of the speaker/reader. The middle-class values Stewart preaches, then, are framed as practices that the women *already* know and already undertake regularly.

Here, Stewart takes what I would call an unethical advantage of the students' isolated position. The *Country Life Readers* employ persuasive efforts precisely because they target large groups of people who already shared common knowledges and methods; to alter these methods required that a majority of men be convinced that the methods were sound or, alternatively, that the benefits of using new, scientific farming methods outweighed the social desire to hold fast to traditional ways. Women, isolated in their homes, had less opportunity to create such shared consensus, and because the lessons themselves are designed to be conducted one-on-one, the female student was effectively outnumbered: the teacher and the textbook spoke in favor of Stewart's methods. The very structure of the text often denies that a viable alternative to Stewart's practices exists. I do not mean to suggest that all women who read *Mother's First Book* followed its suggestions, but Stewart certainly intends to make dissent as difficult as possible by creating a text that grants authority and prestige to middle-class behaviors and little recognition whatsoever—even in a negative sense—for traditional practices.

In most of these coercive lessons, the subject matter is related directly to motherhood and housekeeping, which, given the setting for the lessons, could be taken as universal experiences with which all readers could relate. In the later sections of the book, though, Stewart ventures into topics that require differentiation: because she intends to appeal both to Americanizers and rural women, Stewart creates lessons that address nutrition-related topics in relation to both urban and rural life. In a lesson on the benefits of fresh fruit, Stewart first depicts the urban fruit seller: "Fresh fruit. Fresh fruit. Here is fresh fruit for sale! Come buy for the family!" Students are asked, "Imagine somebody at your door calling out like this. What would you do?" Having presented this urban scene, Stewart suggests, "Or, perhaps, you live on a farm. If so, you must have planted fruit trees of all sorts" (55). She then insists, "Whether in the city or on the farm, we must have fruit" (55). Similarly, the very inclusion of lessons on proper cooking techniques appealed to Americanizers who, as John McClymer explains, were passionately concerned with eliminating the stench of cabbage from immigrants' homes ("Americanization" 98): hence, Stewart includes a lesson that explicitly describes proper ways to cook cabbage (61) and offers other instructions on beneficial (one might say American) eating habits. By presenting explicit appeals to both urban and rural women, Stewart created lessons that spoke to the experiences of a wide variety of women while still promoting middle-class values.

Despite what many scholars now recognize as problematic attempts to impose cultural values on uneducated men and women, Stewart's primers represent a valuable extension of Deweyan theories of experiential education to adult populations. In her insistence that adult students' experiences be taken into account in preparing lessons, she implicitly places a high value on those experiences and their educative value, even as her lessons seek to change future behavior. Furthermore, her lessons achieved success by any standard: students who enrolled in Moonlight Schools, by all extant teacher accounts, rarely failed to complete the course. The reading texts and classroom activities succeeded in maintaining student interest and, given available evidence, also seem to have succeeded in providing students with the ability to carry out simple literacy practices.

Perhaps the most significant addition the Moonlight Schools made to Deweyan pedagogy is the recognition that literacy needs are determined by social setting. Though Stewart's stated goal in producing multiple readers is to create texts that reflect student experience, her larger goal, as outlined in *Moonlight Schools: For the Emancipation of Adult Illiterates*, is to provide students with the tools necessary to engage with their community—to share their "talent" with the world. The various primers indicate Stewart's recognition that the communities students would engage with were varied and that the kinds of words and subject lessons needed to succeed in those communities were likewise variable. Hence, the sample letters in the *Country Life Readers, First Book*, feature newly literate men and women corresponding with distant relatives, a rhetorical situation that responded to the real-world conditions of rural life, particularly in Appalachia, where travel between locations was difficult and increasing industry drew families to new, isolated locations. Yet, the sample letters in *The Indian's First Book* are all framed as letters written by Native Americans to agents from the Bureau of Indian Affairs: because Native Americans were kept in proximity through official government policy, there was less need to correspond with distant relatives, and students' most pressing social need was to campaign for the rights (and money) due to them. Though Stewart herself does not articulate her theory of literacy, the rhetorical framing of the primers makes clear that Stewart recognizes that social conditions ultimately determine what counts—or rather, functions—as being "literate." Because Stewart's own definition of literacy relies on completing the material in the Moonlight Schools reading, her definition of literacy thus takes into account social conditions: a Native American is literate when s/he can compose a letter to the Bureau of Indian Affairs, while an Appalachian becomes literate when s/he can communicate with family members and her/his local community. While Dewey, too, argues that experiential education not only draws from students' social experiences but should also prepare students for future social interaction, Stewart extends this argument beyond actual "actions" and into the realm of language practice: experiential education not only prepares students "to perform those fundamental types of activity which makes civilization what it is" (Dewey, My *Pedagogic* 11), not only to act within their community but also to *communicate* about those actions.

The Americanizers and Student Achievement

While the Americanization movement lacked a single figurehead to develop pedagogy and mold the movement's philosophical approach, prominent Americanization programs and organizations, such as the Ford program, the YMCA, and the Bureau of Naturalization, acted as examples and touchstones for Americanization programs around the country. The slight but significant differences among these prominent programs became the fault lines of the Americanization movement as a whole. The Carnegie Corporation's extensive study of Americanization methods adequately represents the general trends within the Americanization movement in the years immediately preceding its 1920 publication.

The Carnegie study is both an examination of existing practices and a recommendation of best practices for future use. Its primary author, Frank V. Thompson, suggests that teachers must recognize that adults

> are not like children who know but little language and who must therefore be taught verbal expression in association with new objects or experiences as they arise. Our pupils have had children's as well as adults' experiences, so that psychologically the problem of learning English consists for them in associating new symbols, new words, and new sentence structures with old experiences for which they already possess more or less adequate symbols. (187)

In keeping with this philosophy, Thompson insists that "in language the sum of all the parts does not equal the whole" and that "anything is 'simple' which is meaningful, interesting, useful" (191).

Because Thompson recognizes that adults already have a firm under-standing of language and because he suggests that adults must be engaged with material that is "meaningful" and "interesting," he strongly advocates whole-word pedagogies in the Carnegie report. He excoriates teachers who employ phonics-based methods for teaching English to adults, terming one such teacher "cocksure" and "blithely unconscious" of how language actually works (193). However, the results of the Carnegie study suggest that most Americanizers disagreed with Thompson's theories. In particular, Thompson notes "an extraordinary difference of opinion among teachers as to the value of phonics in English instruction for adults" and a "wide diversity in practice" (179). Thompson provides a series of "typical answers" to the question "What use do you make of phonics?"; all of the responses indicate some use of phonics in the adult classroom, and several suggest intensive phonics instruction. One superintendent writes, "A constant use of phonetics. Many learn their *a b c*'s in this class" (179). Another explains that "pupils are drilled until they understand thoroughly the phonetics and then applied on selected words for pronunciation" (179). Still another simply states, "As much as possible" (178). In the example Thompson attacks as "blithely unconscious," the teacher writes, "The alphabet is the basis of the English language, and should be used in forming the words of the beginner's vocabulary. A thorough drill should be given to the sounding of the letters *a, e, i, o, u, w,* and *y,* and the division clearly shown between vowel and consonant letters" (192). By these accounts—and given Thompson's disdain for phonics and his attempts to persuade readers to abandon the method, we should assume that the Carnegie text underrepresents, rather than overrepresents, the use of phonics instruction—the majority of Americanization courses employed some phonics instruction.

Like the Moonlight Schools' adoption of whole-word pedagogies, the Americanizers' adoption of phonics pedagogies seems to reflect the Americanizers' long-term goals for students as much as their belief in the immediate efficacy of phonics instruction for adults. In describing his perception of immigrant needs and the end purpose of education, Thompson writes, "It is obvious that the great mass of immigrants have even less need for writing in English than have native Americans; in teaching them English there cannot be even a pretense that they are to become men of letters and that they must be taught the four forms of discourse" (174). Instead, these students "must know how to write their names and addresses, and how to fill in the black spaces in such commonly used instruments as checks, receipts, and applications for postal and express money orders and the like" (174–75). Because he, like Stewart, saw little educational future for immigrants, Thompson favored a whole-word approach that valued students' immediate success and satisfaction above long-term, advanced achievement.

However, the Americanization movement as a whole was less willing to consign immigrants to lives that encompassed little writing. The rhetoric of the Americanization movement framed literacy as essentially American: the idea that many Americans found limited uses for their literacy went unrecognized. Literacy bore with it the "Anglo-Teutonic conceptions of law, order, and government" (Cubberley 15); democracy itself rested on the practice of literacy. Acknowledging that writing is not necessary for certain members of society would have been to undermine the very idea of "American society" as a democratic institution. Not surprising, Thompson's assertion that writing is not necessary gained little traction in the decade following the Carnegie study.

Whatever their motivations, Americanizers in the 1920s moved away from a utilitarian model of adult literacy, designed simply to make immigrants better manual laborers, and instead toward a model of education that contradicted Thompson's claim: increasingly, immigrants were offered and encouraged to enroll in advanced education programs. Evening high schools, which were open to native students but were targeted toward immigrants, were developed throughout the 1920s, and leading adult educators, including Lewis R. Alderman, suggested that adult literacy education should be understood as but the "foundation work" of a larger program of adult education (Alderman, "Adult Education" 133). The NEA's Department of Immigrant Education changed its name to the Department of Adult Education and to reflect this change in focus broadened its membership statement to include all those who taught adults. Immigrants' presence in the college classroom is also represented in the discourse of college compositionists; Fred Newton Scott, for instance, comments,

> In our impatience with the bad English of our students, we forget that much of it comes out of the melting-pot. It is well to remember that more than twelve millions of our fellow-Americans . . . were born in countries where English is not the native language. . . . The children from these homes attend the public schools, and a considerable proportion of them finish the high-school course. Of these last anyone who is above a certain minimum of intelligence and aptitude, may, in spite of his defects of speech, find his way into a college or university. (464)

Compositionists thus recognized that many of the "problems" that arose in student writing were less symptoms of a decline in writing quality than a function of the fact that many students were composing in their second language, indicating that both immigrants and their children—also a target of Americanizers—were indeed in need of the "four forms of discourse," in spite of Thompson's claim otherwise.

Many Americanizers, both because of their rhetorical focus on democratic life and because of their desire to push immigrants toward advanced education, saw their role as providing a version of literacy instruction that would allow students to participate in public discourse. Some Americanizers, particularly in the 1920s, imagined more for (or, perhaps, demanded more of) their students than the simple acts of reading newspapers and filling out checks. Given this emphasis, it is not surprising that many Americanization courses opted for phonics instruction rather than (or in addition to) whole-word pedagogies. Because phonics seemed to promise a higher level of reading achievement, Americanizers could justify their pedagogies in terms of both individual and social good: students would be provided with more opportunities, and they would be better prepared to contribute to democratic society. That many students dropped out long before achieving any reading or writing skills was beside the point: mere "basic" skills offered society little more than no literacy at all. Only advanced literacy "counted" as fulfilling social needs; producing students who stayed in class but who mastered only simple literacy tasks did not end the threat to democracy that provided the rhetorical exigency for the Americanization movement.

Both the Moonlight Schools and the Americanization movement, then, instantiated a paradoxical relationship between goals and means. The Moonlight Schools valued students' abilities highly, but by selecting a teaching method that would guarantee that most students' abilities could find expression in writing, the schools also ensured that students would not find it easy to advance beyond basic literacy. The Americanizers, conversely, had little respect for student contributions, but by selecting a teaching method that attempted to make immigrants as similar as possible to "real Americans," Americanizers could argue that they provided their students with opportunities for educational advancement and individual achievement.

Just as Americanizers sacrificed the benefits of whole-word pedagogies in engaging students in favor of advancing their long-term goals, they also disregarded the Deweyan suggestion that appealing to student experience could keep students interested in school work. The rhetorical framing of Americanization work disallowed the use of many aspects of Deweyan pedagogy. Because the explicit goal of Americanization work—a goal instantiated in the term "Americanization"—was to inspire (or coerce) immigrants to adopt American ways of doing, speaking, and believing, any pedagogy that suggested celebration or even recognition of immigrants' existing beliefs and experiences would have been perceived as counterproductive. As Thompson details, many Americanization programs sought to minimize even the practical use of the immigrants' native languages in the classroom to facilitate the learning of English. Similarly, despite the seeming connection between the goals of Americanizers and Dewey's emphasis on social life, Americanizers were often reluctant to engage in activities that built community or a sense of social engagement in any tangible sense.[18]

Many Americanizers suggested, in fact, that efforts should be made to *discourage* a sense of community among classmates. One "problem" that prevented assimilation, Americanizers believed, was those "thousands [of immigrants] who live together in 'colonies' in the congested sections of great cities, still holding to the language, customs, and manners they brought with them" (Thorngate 123). Disconnecting immigrants from their peers created a more fertile ground for the seeds of Americanization.

However, some prominent Americanizers, including Thompson, did apply one aspect of Deweyan pedagogy to immigrant lessons: selecting lessons that appealed to the students' interests. As Peter Roberts, a widely respected Americanizer, explains, "The foreign-born is very practical. He wants what is useful. . . . He wants that which he can use in his daily life. The teacher in charge of Americanization work, who knows the work-life of the foreign born, can prepare material to supplement the written lesson which will interest the student" (51). Roberts suggests, for instance, that men involved in copper mining learn "mining terms, the names of tools used, the process of mining, and working regulations" (52). Thompson likewise encouraged teachers to focus on basic lessons, such as the students' names and addresses, because these lessons would respond to students' immediate needs. Much like Stewart, Americanizers recognized the need to give students a clear reason to engage with the class, and developing lessons that responded to immediate needs was one way to create this engagement. Yet, the task facing Americanizers was daunting: unlike Moonlight Schools classes, which took place in rural areas and were often quite small, Americanization classes tended to enroll (initially) a larger number of students who had very little in common, both because of Americanizers' policies encouraging classroom heterogeneity and because of the variety of employment available in urban areas. Developing lessons "useful" to all students was correspondingly difficult. Not surprising, the enrollment statistics produced by contemporary researchers suggest that Americanizers were often unsuccessful in their efforts to maintain students' interest (see Miller; Thompson).

Principles and Motivations

Despite their differences in social and geographical location, student populations, and pedagogical emphases, Americanizers and Moonlight Schools teachers agreed on one core principle: literacy education should prepare students to participate in their society. At a more basic level, they agreed that learning to read and write was necessary for meaningful social participation. And they agreed that this preparation should take into account student interests, if not student aspirations. From these central points of agreement—points of agreement that connote what I call a Deweyan pedagogy—two distinct pedagogical models emerged. By considering the differences in philosophy that led to these disparate pedagogies, I highlight the assumptions underlying in each of these models—models that continue to inform the practice of teaching writing.

One difference is both logical and easily identified: the two groups understood the end points of their work in very different ways. The Moonlight Schools, designed specifically for the least educated adults, aimed for what we might now term "functional literacy": the schools aimed at "nothing more ambitious" than equipping students to function within the modest confines of their immediate, local, often rural, society. While the Americanizers had far less faith in their students' intellectual abilities than Stewart, they also worked much harder to prepare students for advanced educational opportunities—primarily secondary and vocational education but potentially even college-level courses—by selecting models of basic education that mimicked those processes used in secondary and tertiary education.

These end goals reflect a less explicit but no less important difference in the groups' understanding of the nature of social advancement and, by extension, society itself. For the Moonlight Schools, "society" was not totalizing; the social setting of the Appalachian mountains was vastly different from that of a Western reservation, and the Moonlight Schools' pedagogy demanded that teachers take local social conditions into account. Indeed, the Moonlight Schools' emphasis on volunteer teachers (more on this in chapter 4) guaranteed that teachers would be familiar with the social milieu of their students and would therefore be equipped to prepare students to read and write themselves into their local communities. The Moonlight Schools were also more practical: immersed as she was in the society of her first students, Stewart was keenly aware of the difficulty those students would face in achieving anything resembling higher education. In addition to the hindrance of poor educational opportunity, few students could have afforded tuition, fewer still had the means to travel outside the mountains to attend school, and even fewer had the ability to support themselves once there. Similarly, the other groups of students who most inspired Stewart—soldiers, mothers, Native Americans, and African Americans—were prevented by social circumstance, prejudice, and, in many cases, law from attending institutes of higher education. For Stewart, to prepare students for an education they would never have the opportunity to receive would have been cruel, and, as she would have bluntly stated, it would have been a waste of good time and resources that would be better used to provide basic education to those who needed it.

For Americanizers, "society" was equivalent to a universal "American society." Immigrants were perceived as a threat because of their "difference": "they" were not like "us" (in most cases, because "they" could not write and "we" could). This rhetorical framing of the "immigrant problem" and the Americanization solution disallowed a rendering of "society" as a complex, differentiated system that represented a myriad of beliefs, languages, and behaviors: Americanizers imagined one model of patriotism, one model of behavior, and one (English) language. Despite what Michael R. Olneck describes as the role of Americanization in "symbolically construct[ing] or enact[ing] a relationship of benevolent control and social superiority between native and newcomer" (416), the logic of Americanization rhetoric demanded that immigrants (could) become "us"—an "us" that could go to college, could be educated, and could participate in society. For the immigrants to desire something other than advanced education would signify, once again, their difference from middle-class America and indicate the failure of the assimilationist project, recapitulating the threat of difference. At the same time, the *reality* of immigrants receiving a college education—and in doing so, competing with the middle class for jobs and for positions in "American society"—posed no less a threat.

Although the groups disagreed on the end goal of their educational program, both focused on students as adults and on designing coursework appropriate for adult students. Though Americanization teachers, many of whom were not provided with materials or training, often did employ children's primers and lessons with adult students (see Miller), Americanization theorists saw this practice as irresponsible, and they urged additional training that would permit teachers to tailor their lessons to adults (see Miller; Thompson; Roberts). The Moonlight Schools were explicitly designed for adults, and Stewart makes clear that her first priority in designing instructional materials is to account for adults' needs and to differentiate their lessons from those of elementary students. In practice, this means leaving behind those elements of Deweyan pedagogy that demand that the child be understood as a *future* worker, a *future* participant in society. Americanizers and the Moonlight Schools hoped to improve society by teaching students, certainly—but part of the reason that literacy instruction was so necessary stemmed from the fact that students were *already* a part of society. For Americanizers, the illiteracy of immigrants threatened to dilute literate "society"; Stewart also sees illiteracy as promoting social problems, such as feuding, but she believes that illiteracy robs society of great minds and rare talents. In both cases, the men and women being taught are imagined as active participants in society, and it is this very participation that rendered their illiteracy dangerous. Though the Americanizers' and Moonlight Schools' recognition of student agency and intelligence is both admirable and forward-thinking, this attitude also has negative effects: because students were already members of society but members who did not live up to social standards, students could easily be positioned as scapegoats. The Moonlight Schools, which placed a premium on student agency, also tacitly suggests that social problems, such as crime and poverty, are *caused* by illiteracy; if students refuse the "help" the Moonlight Schools offered, the students could be read as willingly encouraging these social ills.

In offering these critiques, I do not mean to suggest that one group created "better" pedagogies than another. Both the Moonlight Schools and the Americanizers made contributions to pedagogical theory that benefited contemporary students and might continue to be of use to modern educators. Both groups attempted to pursue educational methods that they believed would improve their students' lives and economic prospects. And both groups ultimately succeeded in improving social conditions for at least some of their students and in calling attention to the need for a better understanding of students' literacy practices. But both groups also endorsed what modern educators consider deeply problematic assumptions concerning student agency and social good. By acknowledging the assumptions that produced both the beneficial and potentially harmful aspects of each group's pedagogies, we can, moving forward, better gauge the assumptions undergirding our own pedagogical choices and analyze the potential gains and losses those pedagogies might entail for our students.

4. THE POLITICS OF AMERICANIZATION

$\mathcal{E}$o date, research on the history of education has focused heavily on pedagogical practices and theoretical frameworks—that is, activities within the classroom and within academic discourse as represented in scholarly journals. Little research has focused on how literacy education practices have been represented to the public at large, and, indeed, actual pedagogical practices and public representations of those practices have often been conflated. This chapter analyzes the debate between the Moonlight Schools and Americanizers and the struggle that arose from their differing ideological premises. This struggle took place within wider public discourse, particularly at sites of public, rather than exclusively academic, exchange between educators: the meetings of the National Education Association, congressional hearings on educational policy, the headquarters of government agencies and private foundations, and newspaper headlines.

In particular, I examine the rhetorical choices made by both groups in their efforts to represent their own work as worthy and effective and to denigrate the work of the opposing faction. This chapter considers how and why Americanization advocates were able to secure public funding for their efforts, while Stewart and her fellow Moonlight Schools advocates were relatively unsuccessful in finding public or private funding to support their work. I suggest that Stewart's effort to appeal to and subvert the proponents of Americanization by employing a rhetoric of American identity and whiteness was ultimately unsuccessful in sustaining the Moonlight Schools movement; however, I also argue that it is this very effort that makes Stewart's work valuable for modern-day literacy educators. First presented is an overview of Americanization rhetoric and the policies and politics of school funding, and then is an analysis of how Stewart responded to both of these forces in crafting the rhetoric of the Moonlight Schools.

The Rhetoric of Americanization

Beginning in the 1880s, the United States experienced a shift in immigration patterns. In the first century of US history, most immigrants had come from Northern Europe. After 1880, the volume of immigration increased in response to rapid industrialization and the resulting demand for cheap labor. Arriving between 1890 and 1910 were thirteen million immigrants (Carlson 80), most of them Catholic or Jewish and from southern or eastern Europe (Weiss xiii).

ASSIMILATING "NEW" IMMIGRANTS

The drastic change in immigration patterns led to new and expansive efforts to "Americanize" the newcomers. Although this urge to Americanize is, of course, a nativist reaction, it differs substantially from earlier (though equally virulent) responses to perceived threats to native identity. Whereas the influx of immigrants from northern Europe and Ireland in the 1850s and 1860s also spawned organizations designed to counteract the perceived threat immigrants posed, these organizations were rarely educative. As education historian Malcolm Shepard Knowles explains, "Northern and western Europe . . . had educational systems and cultural heritages similar to those of early America," while the new southern European immigrants did not share a common culture, religion, or language with most "native-born" Americans (55). Though definitions of educational status and literacy varied widely near the turn of the century, almost all commentators agreed that the new immigrants were "less educated" and less literate than northern European immigrants (Knowles 56). In his 1919 survey of Americanization courses, Howard Hill provides census data to outline the shift in educational attainment: "Whereas in our earlier immigration the illiteracy of immigrants had occasionally been less than that of native Americans, in 1910, 12.7 per cent of foreign-born were illiterate, against 3 per cent of native Americans" (611). Worse, in Hill's view, was that these immigrants had "customs, habits, and to some extent ideals that formed striking contrasts to those of Northern and Western Europe," and "unlike the earlier immigrants, many of the late-comers manifested . . . no desire of becoming Americans" (611). Ellwood Cubberley, a well-known educator and superintendent of San Francisco, California, schools, declared the new immigrants "illiterate, docile, lacking in self-reliance and initiative, and not possessing the Anglo-Teutonic conceptions of law, order, and government," adding that "their coming has served to dilute tremendously our national stock, and to corrupt our civic life" (Cubberley 15).

In short, the new immigrants were perceived as less desirable than earlier immigrants because they were more difficult to assimilate, even if the immigrants themselves desired to become "100 percent American." As Americanizer Helen Varick Boswell explains, "We have begun to realize that peoples living side by side do not necessarily constitute a nation" (204). Ella Thorngate presented a more hyperbolic image:

> We called America the great "melting-pot" and were satisfied that all this raw material was going through the refining process and would come out as good Americans in time. But much of the raw material never got into the "melting-pot" and has remained *raw material* with all its Europeanism. This is represented by the thousands who live together in "colonies" in the congested sections of great cities, still holding to the language, customs, and manners they brought with them. (123)

For both of these women, as well as the local, state, and federal governments, one answer to the immigrant "threat" was to "Americanize" the offending immigrants by teaching them American values and American ways, including "caring for babies, ventilating the house, [and] preparing American vegetables" (Boswell 206).

As historians Bernard J. Weiss and Robert A. Carlson have separately outlined, Americanization education can be defined in a variety of ways. Carlson defines as Americanizers those who "sought to uphold freedom by indoctrinating norms of belief in religion, politics, and economics" (4). By this definition, Americanization can be said to predate the formation of the United States as a country. Alternatively, Weiss draws on Cubberley to define Americanization as the effort to "assimilate and amalgamate these people [the immigrants] as part of our American race, and to implant in their children, so far as can be done, the Anglo-Saxon conception of righteousness, law and order, and popular government" (xiii). One source of difficulty in establishing a definition through which to examine Americanization courses is the wide scope of definitions operating between

1900 and 1930. Researchers William Sharlip and Albert Owens explain in a 1925 text that "there is little agreement concerning the scope and purpose of Americanization" (12). Sharlip and Owens then offer thirteen unique definitions given by leading commentators of the period and note in particular that there is "no unanimity of opinion as to whether or not the native-born should be embraced within the term *Americanization*" (15). But the definitions also show little agreement as to the role of language. Many avoid referencing language at all, implying, perhaps, agreement with US Supreme Court justice James McReynold's assertion in his 1919 ruling against compulsory English education that "even if the end result of giving all the youth of the nation a knowledge of English was desirable, it still could not be coerced" and, further, that "mere knowledge" of a language other than English "could not now be regarded as harmful" (O'Brien 164). Others, including Theodore Roosevelt and Sharlip and Owens themselves, insisted that fluency in a "common language"—specifically English—was an essential component of Americanization.

Despite this disagreement about the importance of English language to Americanization curriculum, nearly every Americanization course for which records remain included lessons on both speaking and *literacy*, and the overwhelming majority of these lessons were conducted in English. The Bureau of Naturalization's textbook describes a beginner's class, including an elementary reading lesson:

> The teacher sits quietly on a chair before the class and when she has the attention of all, she says, slowly and distinctly, "I sit." She rises, then sits again, and again says, "I sit." . . . She writes *I sit* upon the board. She has the pupils read, "I sit." She points to the sentence, reads it, and sits as she does so. (US Bureau of Naturalization 5)

In the Cleveland Foundation's survey of Americanization courses in the city, Herbert Adolphus Miller gives repeated examples of attempts to teach reading and writing:

> In the first of the five classes [surveyed by one agent] a writing lesson was being conducted, and these husky laboring men were busily engaged in copying, "I am a yellow bird. I can sing. I can fly. I can sing to you." . . . In the fourth room the pupils had a reading lesson about "Little drops of water, Little grains of sand." They then had a spelling lesson of the words in the reading selection. (92–93)

Furthermore, as the Bureau of Naturalization's foray into textbook authorship suggests, nearly all Americanization classes relied on a textbook of some sort, either drawn from children's lessons or designed specifically for work with immigrant adults. The use of these textbooks, perhaps more than any specific lesson plan, suggests the centrality of reading lessons in Americanization courses.

The emphasis on teaching reading and, to a lesser extent, writing indicates a widespread belief among Americanizers and their supporters—including government officials—that the "common language" of America was both a spoken and a *written* English. Thorngate, for instance, lamented the revelation that over one-third of World War I draftees could not read well enough to take a standard paper-and-pencil exam: "Of the 8,500,000 immigrants and native illiterates over ten years of age, 5,500,000 could not read or write English. Even in our own city, Omaha, they say there are 5,000 people who cannot read or write English, and English is the language of the United States of America!" (124). Thorngate here elides the distinction between spoken language fluency and literacy skills; to know the "language of the United States of America" is to be able to read and write English, not to speak it. In 1906, researcher Grover Huebner makes a similar rhetorical move, disclaiming, on the one hand, the linkage between literacy and American identity while, on the other, using literacy as a measure of Americanization: "While it is not claimed that an illiterate man is not an American and that a literate man is, it does indicate whether or not the school has influenced him. It is safe to say that if the school has changed the child from a condition of illiteracy to one of literacy he has been Americanized to a large extent" (199). In the rhetoric of many Americanizers, illiteracy (in fact or in perception) came to symbolize "un-American" identity, and its removal was a significant marker of assimilation.

Other educators argue that if spoken English fluency is the goal of Americanization, literacy in any language would further this aim: "Perhaps the most serious difficulty in the way of teaching the English language," education advocate Carol Aronovici opines, "is the illiteracy of many of the immigrants in this country" (712).[1] Literacy skills, these theorists suggest, improve one's ability to comprehend the structure of language, thus improving one's ability to acquire a second language. Most frequently, however, calls for literacy teaching had a far less scientific or practical foundation: Americanizers advocated literacy education primarily in terms of assimilation. Illiteracy is a marker of foreignness; therefore, eliminating illiteracy became in many ways synonymous with eliminating foreign thoughts, languages, and beliefs.

Perhaps because of its connection to English-language teaching, Americanization is often perceived as a response to anti-German World War I propaganda. However, both Knowles and Kett emphasize that Americanization courses gained popularity prior to the war. In 1906, Huebner outlined what schools, trade unions, and churches were *already* doing to promote the Americanization of immigrants. As Carlson details, Jane Addams and John Dewey had advocated more humanistic versions of Americanization throughout the first decade of the century:

> Dewey and the settlement workers wanted the schools to be, in the words of Jane Addams, "a socializing and harmonizing factor" in American society. Dewey described the settlements, like the schools he desired, as "bringing people together, of doing away with barriers of caste, or class, or race, or type of experience . . ." They were echoing the cry of the Americanizers. (87)

Given the development of Americanization programs at least as early as the 1890s, these courses have a claim to be the first organized adult literacy education program.

WORLD WAR I: AMERICANIZATION AS DEFENSE

Though Americanization programs predate World War I, the war did give the Americanization movement a new sense of urgency. As McClymer explains, during the war, "[d]iversity smacked of disloyalty" ("Americanization" 97). He credits Theodore Roosevelt as playing a "key role" in promoting the idea of "100 percent Americanism" ("Americanization" 97), and Roosevelt's rhetoric was indeed passionately pro-"American": in 1916, he declared that "unless the immigrant becomes in good faith an American and nothing else, then he is out of place in this country, and the sooner he leaves the better" and warned against "the evil intrigues of these hyphenated Americans" (Roosevelt 77; 101). But Roosevelt was not the only advocate of absolute patriotism; Woodrow Wilson and members of his administration, particularly the Bureau of Naturalization, also pressed forward the image of 100 percent Americanism. The bureau "came to see citizenship training not simply as a useful service to those seeking naturalization but as a vital component of the nation's internal security" (McClymer, "Americanization" 99). The National Americanization Committee (NAC) (led by vice-chairman Frances Kellor, perhaps the most widely known proponent of Americanization). one of the more powerful groups that sought to organize Americanization efforts,

> initially presented Americanization in terms of mutual obligations: the foreign-born would adopt the English language and American ways, and the native–born would accept the immigrants as equal partners in a common destiny. When the country entered the war in 1917, the NAC turned over nearly its entire staff and equipment to the national government. At that point, the group's rhetoric became more overtly nationalistic. (Salomone 31–32)

The war pushed existing Americanization programs toward more intense education efforts and toward an increased emphasis on the markers that signified identifiable "Americanness." As such, English-language teaching gained traction as the essential element of Americanization courses.

But the war changed Americanization courses—and adult education in general—in a more significant way. Because Americanization was seen as an issue of national security, it became much easier for supporters to gain public funding for classes. As Hill states, "Prior to 1914 . . . the only state in the Union which had made financial provision for the education of immigrants was New Jersey" (619). But by 1915, "eleven states had made appropriations for the support of evening schools" for immigrants (621). Hill also records funding from local sources; Cleveland's local government "appropriated a sum sufficient to defray all expenses of these special classes [for immigrants]" (622). Frank Cody details similar funding in Detroit: "Three years ago [in 1916], the appropriation for evening schools was $65,000, last year it was $95,000, and this year [1918] it is $100,000" (618). While long-standing federal resistance to funding education prevented a direct appropriation from the federal government toward the support of Americanization courses, the Bureau of Naturalization used "its surplus revenues . . . to print and distribute its citizenship textbook to aliens who were petitioning for naturalization and attending public school programs" (McClymer, "Americanization" 101). The bureau later undertook a survey of "publicly supported Americanization work" (102). Though McClymer demonstrates that the enrollment figures the bureau calculates are not reliable because many classes listed had been shut down—usually due to lack of interest from students—and others had underreported the number of immigrants enrolled in classes, what the bureau's data show is that 2,872 cities and towns had at some point between 1914 and 1922 appropriated public funds to Americanization work, whether or not those funds were actually used (102–3).

In Americanization rhetoric, public funding was not premised on morality or compassion but rather cultural and even racial defense; Americanization rhetoric was often accompanied, for instance, by warnings against Anglo-Saxon "race suicide" (Roediger). Funding appeals were linked not primarily to the good of immigrants—though this appeal was often included—but the good of society as a whole. Immigrants were not depicted as "deserving" instruction, and the fact that courses were free was not framed as stemming from a belief in the right of all people to education. Instead, immigrants were portrayed as being unwilling or unable to pay for fee-based courses, and their education was justified as a public necessity; failure to educate immigrants might result in nothing less than the complete collapse of democratic institutions.

As historian James R. Barrett explains, Americanization, particularly during World War I, typically meant "something the native middle class did to immigrants, a coercive process by which elites pressed WASP values on immigrant workers, a form of social control" (997). Americanization was not—except in rare cases, such as Addams's Hull House—a student-centered enterprise but one that sought to perpetuate social hierarchies through education. Michael R. Olneck asserts that

> the significance of the Americanization movement need not . . . rest on its effect on the behavior, thought, and identifications of the immigrants it sought to transform. Rather, . . . Americanization may be interpreted as "symbolic behavior," which is "ritualistic and ceremonial in that the goal is reached in the behavior itself rather than in any state which it brings about." . . . Not only did the content of the Americanizers' rhetoric, texts, and rituals symbolically assign status to those adhering most closely to the culture of native-born Americans. The activity of Americanizing the immigrants also assigned to native-born Americans the roles of tutor, interpreter, and gatekeeper, while rendering immigrants the subjects of tutelage and judgment. Doing Americanization symbolically constructed or enacted a relationship of benevolent control and social superiority between native and newcomer. (399; 416)

A key part of the symbolically constructed social superiority Americanizers enacted was the attribution of illiteracy to the foreign-born. To complete the symbolic relationship created by the rhetoric of Americanization, the reality that "new" immigrants had higher levels of illiteracy than "old" immigrants or than native Americans was totalized to create an us/them binary: immigrants *as a group* were figured as illiterate, and white native-born citizens were depicted as literate. An exchange from the *Congressional Record* of 1914 aptly demonstrates the tenor of this rhetoric:

> Mr. KELLEY of Michigan. I notice from the report issued by the Commissioner of Education that out of every thousand white people in the State of Texas there are forty-three over 10 years of age who can not read or write.
> Mr. DIES. Very likely that is true. . . . I will tell you how we got that. You set the negroes free, and you neglected to educate them. You set them free for us to educate, and we are taxing ourselves every year, and we are doing it the best we can and getting along nicely. The illiteracy the gentleman speaks of is the illiteracy among the colored people.
> Mr. KELLEY of Michigan. But this report says that forty-three out of every thousand white people are illiterate.
> Mr. DIES. Oh, well, then, there is more immigration from foreign countries into Texas than I imagined there was. [*Laughter.*] (4192)

As the war progressed, more and more congressmen adopted Mr. Dies's attitude; by 1917, Congress passed a bill requiring a reading test for all immigrants over President Wilson's veto. With this bill, official government policy codified the relationship between reading ability and American values: if one could not already read, one clearly did not possess the character necessary to be an American.

The force of this symbolic binary uniting literacy and American identity boded ill for the Moonlight Schools, because the binary insisted on a connection between literacy and American identity. If one was not literate, this characterization implied, one could not be American. Native-born illiterates were thus othered by a symbolic process constructed to conserve native identity. Their American identity—and by extension, their racial and ethnic identity as white—was symbolically denied due to their illiteracy. Yet, the practicality of material resources and funding required that Stewart and the Moonlight Schools become part of the conversation surrounding Americanization and that efforts to teach native illiterates be cast in relation to the rhetoric of American identity.

The Realities of School Funding

The initial student population of the Moonlight Schools was made up of Appalachians. This starting point to some extent occurred by happenstance—Stewart had lived in eastern Kentucky throughout her life, and her work was inspired by the conditions she encountered there. These conditions, though, were not happenstance but, rather, a product of educational districting and funding policies that had long made rural education a daunting if not impossible proposition. By 1910, the year prior to the first Moonlight School session, rural education was widely characterized as inefficient and ineffective—in fact, conditions almost guaranteed a continuing population of adult illiterates, because even if compulsory attendance laws were enforced, the one-room schoolhouse often could not provide adequate educational opportunities for all the students it served.

The *Addresses and Proceedings* of annual NEA meetings provide a record of mounting concerns surrounding rural education. In fact, the NEA established a Department of Rural and Agricultural Education in 1908 to explore the unique issues and challenges facing rural schools. In spite of the existence of this department, discussions of rural education reform spill over into the proceedings of almost every other department. Though an almost mind-boggling number of issues are addressed by rural school advocates, three primary concerns regarding rural education recur throughout the *Addresses and Proceedings* between 1910 and 1915: lack of funding, lack of parental support for education, and lack of teacher training and interest.

Of these concerns, Stewart was most keenly aware of the lack of funding available for rural schools. As Rowan County school superintendent, one of her tasks was to assess the equipment each school in her district possessed. These accounts, preserved in her papers, include counts of desks, chalkboards, and even windows and window dressings. None of these items were in adequate supply in Stewart's schools. As Baldwin describes, the "per capita expenditure per child [in Rowan County] was $4.36, one-fifth the national average" (23), providing little opportunity to upgrade or even replenish supplies. Stewart was in charge of dispersing the meager funds available to the schools, and she was thus aware of both the dearth of supplies available to rural teachers and the dearth of money available to the school board for remedying the problem. However, she was also aware of the near impossibility of obtaining any increase in funding in the foreseeable future.

The chief cause of poor funding for rural schools resulted from well-entrenched laws stipulating that local schools should be funded by local taxation. In poor districts, voters refused to apportion adequate money to schools. Furthermore, individuals in these communities did not have the income to pay for adequate schools, even if such taxes had existed. As educator Warren Wilson reported to the NEA in 1912,

> [I]f you believe that farmers have an adequate income, I refer you to the survey recently made at Cornell University, which showed that the farmers around that splendid institution, devoted to helping the farmer get up, get an income of less than $1.20 per day for their work. . . . I begin to believe, for my part, what the farmer says when we go to him to propose the improvement of schools or churches or roads in the country. His reply is: "I cannot afford it," and I cannot but believe that the farmer is telling the truth. (283)

The lack of funding was exacerbated by the number of rural schools. In spite of lower population density, rural areas often supported as many schools as urban districts. Poor or absent roads meant that students could not travel easily to distant schools; as a result, each small community supported its own one-room schoolhouse.[2]

City schools were funded at much-higher rates than rural schools. Though poverty existed in cities as well, wealth was also concentrated in cities, creating a larger tax base from which to fund an almost equal number of schools. As speaker D. W. Hayes reported at the 1913 annual meeting,

> While but little more than one-third of the children of the United States are in city schools, there has been expended toward their education 55 per cent of all the moneys expended for education. Putting it another way: nearly two-thirds of the children of the United States are in rural schools, while but little more than 45 per cent of the money invested in public education is expended for the maintenance of rural schools. (546)

This difference in school funding was reflected in illiteracy statistics: 10 percent of rural people were illiterate, according to the 1910 census,[3] while only 5 percent of urban residents were illiterate. The census abstract further highlights the differences in urban and rural illiteracy: "The contrast between urban and rural illiteracy is by far the greatest in the case of native whites of native parentage, of whom less than 1 per cent were illiterate in urban communities and over 5 per cent in rural districts. There was also a much higher percentage of illiteracy among the negroes in rural districts than in urban communities" (US Bureau of the Census, *Thirteenth . . . Abstract* 73). These statistics suggest that when immigrants were omitted from statistical consideration, the division among urban and rural people who had been educated (or who had *not* been educated) in the United States was striking: rural native whites were five times more likely to be illiterate than urban native whites.

The poor conditions of rural schools both arose from and reflected local parents' attitudes toward education. Wilson relates, "Henry C. Wallace, of Des Moines, recently declared that in the state of Iowa the profit on farms was measured by the child labor put on the farms. In the city we think it disgraceful that a child should work, but in such a rich state as Iowa the farmer's only source of income in average instances is the labor of children" (283). The status of children as workers on rural farms created a double bind for rural school reformers: if compulsory education laws succeeded in bringing these children into school, their presence in schools would concomitantly lower the tax base funding the schools, leading to poorer educational standards.

In particular, the lack of funding led to poor teaching. As Wilson's study reveals, "In Georgia 88 per cent last year of the country school-teachers were each teaching for the first time in that school" (284). High teacher turnover and low teacher training resulted from the poor salaries rural schools offered; one of the NEA's most frequently advocated "solutions" for the problem of rural schools was a salary scale "based on years of service, so that for at least five years the most rural schools would pay its teacher the same salary as is paid in the most central of city schools" (Keppel 719). Many farmers were not willing to sacrifice the income their children represented for the substandard education provided in "poorly heated, poorly lighted, poorly ventilated, and poorly taught" schools (De Garmo 304). The poor quality of rural schools and the illiteracy that resulted were self-perpetuating: parents who had not received a worthwhile education from rural schools were unwilling to support those schools, thus denying their children the opportunity to be educated.

The first students of the Moonlight Schools were white Appalachians, who were particularly subject to the poor schooling conditions rural school advocates outlined because of the absence of infrastructure connecting isolated rural communities. Though Kentucky's 1909 education reform bill sought to alleviate the problem of rural school funding by consolidating school districts, by 1911, the year Stewart founded the Moonlight Schools, consolidation had gained little traction in eastern Kentucky because students simply could not travel long distances to consolidated schools. Additionally, eastern Kentucky teaching jobs were among the least desirable because of the lack of funding for supplies and the lack of infrastructure; those who agreed to teach were either local women in search of (any) work or poor teachers who could not find work elsewhere.

The 1910 census data for Kentucky reflect these schooling conditions: while the national average for rural illiteracy was 10.1 percent, 12.1 percent of all Kentuckians were illiterate. Almost 12 percent of native white Kentuckians were illiterate—more than double the national average even for rural white illiteracy and twelve times more than urban native whites. But even these statistics do not adequately represent the divide between Appalachian education and education in other areas, urban or rural. Appalachian counties posted the highest illiteracy rates in the state: of the fifty-three Kentucky counties the Appalachian Regional Commission designated as Appalachian,[4] thirty-four reported illiteracy rates higher than 15 percent in the 1910 census,[5] and of these, seventeen counties reported illiteracy rates higher than 20 percent.

Initially, then, Stewart understood illiteracy as a product of rural schooling practices; the people who came to her office to have her read their letters were not men and women who had "frittered away" their opportunity for education but men and women who had "never had a chance" to learn (Stewart, "Illiteracy as a Factor" 52). As she explains in *Moonlight Schools: For the Emancipation of Adult Illiterates*, "Many of these people had never been permitted, for reasons all too tragic, to enter school, or if enrolled, they had been stopped at the end of a week, a month or at the close of their first term" (4). The Moonlight Schools were a way, as described elsewhere in this volume, for Stewart to both repair past injustices of the rural school and improve its future prospects. If parents could see the value of education, they would be more likely to support the school, both by levying tax-based appropriations for the school and by allowing their children to attend regularly. Though Stewart also campaigned for other varieties of rural school improvement, particularly legislation that sought to improve teacher salaries and place schools under state and federal jurisdiction, she believed the most immediate solution to the problems facing rural schools was to bring education to adults. Though holding Moonlight Schools in local schoolhouses was primarily practical, it was also symbolic—the schools were the site where past educational injustices were rectified, imbuing both the school building and the teachers it housed with positive connotations.

Americanization Funding Rhetoric: Invoking Native White Identity

Stewart founded the Moonlight Schools amidst an upsurge in attention to adult illiteracy. Given that the Moonlight Schools' spread through the United States coincided with the largest outcry supporting public funding for adult education in US history, one might assume that the Moonlight Schools benefited from this explosion of available money. However, throughout her career as a literacy advocate, Stewart spent the vast majority of her time seeking funding to carry on Moonlight Schools and never received more than $32,250 of public funds per year for her literacy programs. In 1916, Stewart received $5,000 with which to organize adult literacy education for the entire state of Kentucky; in the same year, Cody attests that the city of Detroit alone appropriated $65,000 for Americanization courses aimed at adults (618).

At both the local and state levels, the lack of funding for Moonlight Schools as compared to the funding given to Americanization programs reflected the disparity of educational funding between rural and city schools. During the Kentucky Illiteracy Commission's 1919 campaign, Stewart asked speakers to emphasize education funding statistics; as Baldwin details, "Audiences across the state were told Kentucky's $977 per capita income was nearly $1,000 lower than the national figure of $1,965, and that its per pupil expenditure of $9.76 was less than half the nation's average of $22.76" (115). Given that so little funding was available even for traditional students, Stewart expected and received little aid from state and local sources.

In the absence of this funding, Stewart appealed primarily to two other sources for financing: private clubs and the federal government. Both of these audiences were, during the period of Stewart's work, keenly focused on Americanization. Nearly all of Stewart's rhetorical efforts between the years 1914 and 1925 can be read as a response to the dominant discourse of adult education at the time: the discourse of Americanization. Stewart's response was nuanced: because she relied on Americanization supporters for funding, she invoked many of the tropes of the movement in her speeches and writing—yet, Stewart also resisted the totalizing discourse surrounding literacy that was a hallmark of Americanization as she sought to redefine illiteracy as a marker of governmental refusal or inability to provide adequate educational opportunities rather than as a marker of personal failure or moral ineptitude.

That Stewart's rhetoric was directed at Americanization supporters is evident in the introduction to *Moonlight Schools: For the Emancipation of Adult Illiterates*. In the text, Stewart draws on William Goodell Frost's rhetoric to mark a clear contrast between native illiterate mountaineers and foreign-born illiterates by emphasizing Appalachian culture as a "reservoir of strength and patriotism" (5). Like many reformers of the time, Stewart took advantage of the image of Appalachia "invented" by nineteenth-century local-color writers that called forth a region of blood feuds, backwardness, and extreme poverty (Shapiro). As historian Allen Batteau reminds us, "tens of thousands of high-minded citizens have been galvanized to action, millions of words have poured forth from journalists and novelists, and billions of dollars in federal programs have been spent" (6) both to support these stereotypes and to attempt to resolve these identified "problems." Rather than denying these stereotypes, Stewart acknowledges Appalachian "backwardness" but celebrates it as a uniquely preserved national heritage rather than a bastion of ignorance; for instance:

> [It is] comforting to remember that in these mountains of the southern states America has a reservoir of strength and patriotism in the millions of pure Anglo-Saxon Americans. . . . [I]t should be developed and permitted to send its strength to every section to carry virility and the very essence of Americanism to communities where these precious things are diluted or dying out. (5–7)

The defining characteristic of Appalachians—the "strongest urge of the mountaineer's soul"—is "his eager, hungry, insatiable desire for knowledge" (3). Stewart acknowledges that Appalachians have been "deprived for years of educational opportunities" but insists that "they have not degenerated" (3) and are still quite capable of learning. Because local-color writers had been largely responsible for creating the image of Appalachians as "peculiar" or "backward," Stewart speaks explicitly to these misconceptions: "Of all the authors who have chosen them as their theme and the artists who have recently begun to present them as a type, none have seemed to catch, or at least have failed to portray" the desire for education that Appalachians possessed (3). While acknowledging that Appalachians are to some degree uncivilized—they only "stand at the threshold of a new civilization" (5) but are not yet a part of that civilization—Stewart suggests that it is a simple matter to improve their condition: "They need the world's help, its best thought, its modern conveniences" (5) only to become as civilized as any other section of the country.

The hyperbolic and nativist celebration of Appalachian people in *Moonlight Schools* depicts the schools as a racist enterprise, designed to fortify white racial identity. Robert A. Luke points out,

> In Cora Wilson Stewart's story of the Moonlight Schools in Eastern Kentucky in the second decade of this century there is no reference to work among the blacks. . . . Of the 26 fine, rare photographs in the book, all are of Caucasian groups and all of "whites of the South" except one of "Mexican mothers in California learning to read and write" and another of immigrant "Jewish mothers in New York improving their education." (xvii)

The images Luke cites of Mexican mothers is particularly noteworthy, as the women in the image appear to be more white than the mountaineers featured in other pictures—that is, the images emphasize the similarities between these women and native white students. Only one reference is made to black students in the text of the book, while "Anglo-Saxon" people are continually described as students of the highest caliber. *Moonlight Schools* leaves its reader with the impression that the schools are exclusively a "white" enterprise.

However, archival evidence suggests that the framing of whiteness and American identity in *Moonlight Schools* is a rhetorical strategy rather than an accurate reflection of the Moonlight Schools' practices. From the outset of the schools, classes were held in both black and white school districts (though the schools themselves remained segregated). Nelms writes that "some [Kentucky Illiteracy Commission] agents reported their greatest successes among the African-American population" (91). Baldwin asserts that by 1915, "at least fifteen Kentucky counties conducted schools for black students" (49). In addition, these schools employed both "black and white teachers" (Baldwin 137). The Kentucky Illiteracy Commission appointed an advocate to address black school districts. Though no pictures of African American students appear in *Moonlight Schools*, such pictures are included in Stewart's collection of photographs (and some can be viewed in Baldwin's biography). Given the records Stewart kept of African American Moonlight Schools, their existence could easily have been acknowledged or even celebrated in *Moonlight Schools*, yet Stewart chose to omit these references from the published text. Furthermore, Stewart often referenced African American students in her speeches (more on this below), suggesting that her choice to elide African Americans from her published text is a deliberate rhetorical move (see, for example, "Delivered").

Stewart also dedicated a great deal of her time to calling attention to illiteracy among American Indians, though there is no reference to this work in *Moonlight Schools: For the Emancipation of Adult Illiterates*. In 1921, Stewart toured North Dakota reservations to observe educational conditions and develop strategies for teaching literacy to Native Americans. Drawing from the information gathered on these visits, Stewart created *The Indian's First Book*, a primer designed for use in reservation Moonlight Schools. She also persuaded the Northwest Indian Congress to "take a stand for the removal of illiteracy as the first step in a program of Indian welfare and development" (Nelms 143). In 1931, Stewart personally taught a Moonlight School at the Heart Butte Blackfoot reservation. Though much of this work with American Indian populations postdates the publication of *Moonlight Schools*, Stewart had already begun composing *The Indian's First Book*; given Stewart's penchant for well-timed publicity, *Moonlight Schools* represents an excellent opportunity to publicize this upcoming text—yet she makes no mention whatsoever of American Indians in *Moonlight Schools*.

The frequency of Moonlight Schools programs among nonwhite student populations suggests that the white-only image presented in *Moonlight Schools* was a carefully framed rhetorical appeal to (white) readers' sense of racial superiority. The rationale for invoking the Appalachian as the ideal of white American identity can be seen in the clause that precedes Stewart's celebration of "millions of pure Anglo-Saxon Americans": "In a day when racial groups weld themselves together in America and seek to advance the welfare of the country from which they came rather than the welfare of the nation that has received them into its bosom" (*Moonlight Schools: . . . Illiterates* 5). That is, Stewart frames Appalachians as an opposing, conservative (or preservative) force that serves to counterbalance "racialized"—that is, nonwhite—immigrants by emphasizing their status as both "white" and "pure" and, even more important, as "native." In doing so, Stewart echoes the rhetoric of the Americanization movement, which suggests that the recent influx of "unassimilated" immigrants was a threat to American identity. However, Stewart also presents images and accounts of immigrants who have learned to read and write English through the Moonlight Schools. Within its 194 pages, *Moonlight Schools: For the Emancipation of Adult Illiterates* both perpetuates the image of the "new" immigrant as a threat and presents a "solution" to that threat: the Moonlight Schools, she suggests, are an excellent site for assimilation.

Stewart's use of nativist rhetoric appeals directly to Americanization proponents by invoking immigrants as a potential threat and by highlighting native Appalachians as a source of cultural defense and preservation. Americanizers had far greater access to funding than rural school districts; by tailoring her appeal to Americanizers, Stewart could hope to gain access to these funds. She makes the differential in spending on native and immigrant adults a key point in many of her speeches; for instance, in a speech to the Kansas State Teachers Association, Stewart directs this question to "superintendents of rural as well as of city schools":

> Is there any reason why the night school should be a city product and a city institution only? The illiterate foreigner may find the night school open to him in any city where he may land. Then, is there any excuse for condemning our pure-blooded Anglo-Saxon mountaineers, our American farmers and our Western pioneers who did not have an opportunity in childhood, to everlasting ignorance? ("Moonlight" 14)[6]

City night schools were held in public schools and supported by *public funds*; furthermore, the Bureau of Naturalization provided textbooks and pedagogical information free of charge to night schools that educated immigrants. Given the lack of funding even for day school work in the rural communities Moonlight Schools targeted, Stewart had to rely on volunteer teaching and private donations to keep the schools running. She calls attention to this lack of funding subtly throughout *Moonlight Schools: For the Emancipation of Adult Illiterates*; for instance, she writes that giving each newly literate student a Bible was "an offer that was made when our vision was small. . . . When hundreds began to claim it, we tried to keep the faith, and some of us have not yet recovered from the strain on our pocketbooks" (51). By framing the Moonlight Schools as teaching "real Americans"—specifically, Appalachians—Stewart hoped that she could gain access to the public funds and assistance available for "Americanization" efforts.

Though Stewart advocated throughout her work that the best teaching methods involved lessons that were intimately related to the students' daily lives, she also recognized that very few Moonlight Schools organizers could actually afford to buy her textbooks; to create the funds needed to distribute the textbooks to the students they had been designed for, Stewart needed to tap the funding for Americanization classes as a potential revenue stream. As such, her later books, including *Moonlight Schools*, both directly and indirectly appeal to Americanizers. The preface of the *Country Life Readers: Second Book* includes the assertion that "while designed to be used by adults in the moonlight schools, this book is not unsuitable for adults in cities, for they need to become better acquainted with country life and its opportunities. It may also be used to advantage by children in both country and city schools" (3).

Furthermore, many Americanizers were particularly concerned with the illiteracy and un-American ideals of immigrant mothers, because, as the Bureau of Naturalization explained, mothers "have much of the responsibility of determining what kind of citizens their children shall become" (McClymer, "Gender" 10). In response to this focus, Stewart's *Mother's First Book* marks the major themes of Americanization for immigrant women: volunteers who teach mothers in their homes render not just a useful but a "patriotic" service (5), and lessons include appropriate cooking methods. As McClymer explains, an "antipathy to cabbage may seem too outré to be representative of the general run of Americanizers' concerns. In fact, it was typical of them" and their concerns regarding the "American ways of . . . preparing American vegetables, instead of the inevitable cabbage" (Boswell 206).[7] Stewart's lessons, then, on "a new way to cook cabbage . . . about twenty minutes in very little water" or the importance of eating fruit "[w]hether in the city or on the farm" respond to Americanizers' fixation on the daily habits of immigrant women, making the textbook marketable to these comparatively well-funded educators (*Mother's* 61, 55).[8] Similarly, the pictures of "Mexican mothers" and "Jewish mothers" in *Moonlight Schools* emphasize that the Moonlight Schools curriculum is applicable to illiterate immigrant women.[9]

Stewart's texts constructed an argument not only of cultural but of racial defense. As David R. Roediger explains, eastern and southern Europeans were not perceived as "white"; influential sociologist Edward A. Ross, Roediger states, "used the language of race to draw lines between 'Asiatics' and whites but also policed divisions among European groups we would today regard as clearly white" (7). Similarly, the "invention" of Appalachia and its people involved a dualistic denigration and celebration of Appalachian culture. Local-color writers and, in their wake, politicians and reformers revived "the idea of the Anglo-Saxon race as a distinct, all-encompassing force" and as "the purest of the pure" (Horsman 209, 210). Appalachian "backwardness" was imagined to have preserved a now-lost racial heritage and identity. Stewart draws on this image of Appalachia as a bastion of white identity to frame the Moonlight Schools as a counter to the "race suicide" decried by Roosevelt and other Americanizers. This appeal to racial identity also explains the omission Luke notes in *Moonlight Schools: For the Emancipation of Adult Illiterates*: had Stewart highlighted her work with African Americans or American Indians, she would have undercut her case for the Moonlight Schools as a racially conservative enterprise. Also, and perhaps more important, emphasizing the Moonlight Schools' work with nonwhite people would have perpetuated the synonymy of "illiteracy" and "nonwhite," and, by inference, would have undercut the illiterate mountaineer's status as "white."

Rhetorical Resistance to Americanization

In spite of her efforts to appeal to Americanizers (or, more specifically, to their pocketbooks), Stewart was, in fact, staunchly opposed to many of the tenets of the Americanization movement. Though she might easily have tapped into Americanization funding by directly marketing the Moonlight Schools as an Americanization pedagogy, Stewart refused repeatedly to join forces with Americanizers, most notably by refusing to become a member of the Department of Immigrant Education, despite that department's increasingly vital role in sponsoring adult education.[10] Instead, she emphasized the differences between her movement and what she called "immigrant education" and attempted to highlight what she saw as the flaws in the movement without alienating potentially important financial backers. To do this, Stewart focused on two particular misconceptions underpinning the Americanization movement: the idea that illiteracy was in some way "un-American" and the perception that immigrants were largely illiterate and constituted the majority of illiterate people in the United States.

Though Stewart's emphasis on Appalachian whiteness serves to appeal to Americanizers on the grounds of racial defense, the opening of *Moonlight Schools: For the Emancipation of Adult Illiterates* also emphasizes that, though illiterate, Appalachians were quintessentially American. She includes below her own reference to their Anglo-Saxon purity a lengthy footnote that excerpts Roosevelt's *Winning of the West*. In this quotation, Roosevelt describes Appalachians as "a peculiar and characteristically American people" (5) and emphasizes both that they were "Americans by birth and by parentage" (6) and that their immigrant ancestors "were fitted to be Americans from the very start" (7). In public speeches, she refers to the problem of "America's illiteracy" and tells her audiences that "America calls today to her public school teachers to enlist and strike a death-blow at illiteracy" ("Moonlight" 12). She also refers in *Moonlight Schools: For the Emancipation of Adult Illiterates* to the "illiterate soldiers [who] are courageous and patriotic as their understanding will permit" (23). Moreover, though she avoids linking "white" illiteracy to other racial groups in print, she frequently invokes the lack of geographical and racial boundaries on illiteracy in her speeches, for example:

> These schools minister equally to illiterate Indians in Oklahoma, illiterate negroes in Alabama and illiterate white persons in lowland and highland in North Carolina and the other states. California and New Mexico, the last states to adopt the institution, are finding it useful, in the education of the immigrant population of the one, and the large Mexican population of the other. ("Moonlight" 11)

Here, Stewart illustrates that illiteracy knows no bounds of geography or of race—it is a universal problem. Because every region Stewart visited had a unique illiterate population, she needed to emphasize the efficacy of the schools for *all* potential student populations. This changed emphasis between printed texts and public speeches can also be attributed to Stewart's near obsession with fundraising: she was typically paid or contracted for a set speaking fee prior to her performance, so she could feel freer to express her opinions. The books, however, needed to be marketable to a mass audience to be profitable, and their rhetoric is correspondingly more conservative.

Stewart's speeches likewise vary in tone depending on her audience. Because speeches given at the NEA's annual meeting were published in the widely distributed *Addresses and Proceedings*, these speeches are more conservative than those given to private clubs or teachers' organizations. In NEA speeches, Stewart seeks to represent her program in ways that cater to Americanization advocates, who made up a substantial number of the speakers at the annual conferences between 1915 and 1925. Even in this forum, though, Stewart takes advantage of opportunities to highlight the false logic of Americanization. At the 1918 meeting, Stewart states, "Among our five and a half million illiterates, one million, six hundred thousand are foreign born. The remainder, nearly four million in number, are native born. We are attempting to Americanize foreigners, an excellent thing to do, but let us not forget to Americanize the people of the Abraham Lincoln and Booker T. Washington type" ("War-Modified" 119). Here, Stewart credits the work of Americanization with foreigners and appears to offer support for those who, like Sharlip and Owens, would extend Americanization to native-born citizens. However, her references to Abraham Lincoln and Booker T. Washington are tongue-in-cheek—her decision to invoke these two widely respected symbols of patriotism, rather than more generic or less admirable figures, invites the question: who are we to suggest that Lincoln and Washington *need* to be Americanized? Moreover, by suggesting that Lincoln and Washington themselves are of the "type" that need instruction, Stewart highlights that American values exist independent of one's status as literate and educated. Stewart also chooses both a white and a black American as representatives of native American populations, perhaps reminding her audience that African Americans are both educable and worthy of being educated.

Perhaps most telling, Stewart disliked using the term "Americanization" even to characterize education programs designed for immigrants. In her private correspondence, she consistently employs the term "immigrant education" (see, for example, Stewart, Letter to A. E. Winship; Baldwin 156). While Stewart did sometimes employ the term "Americanization" in speeches and letters addressed to Americanization supporters, she uses the term when issuing explicit (though often subtle) critiques of the movement. Stewart believed that "the United States of America is a place where illiterates should meet with instruction, not exclusion," and she supported

Wilson's veto of the literacy test (*School Journal*). For Stewart—and, in fact, for nearly all Americanizers—the term "Americanization" suggested that the essential quality required to be an American was education. By extension, the term implied that uneducated Appalachians were not Americans—on the basis of their lack of an education that America itself had failed to provide them. Fully aware of this paradox, Stewart believed, as Wilson did, that it was both absurd and in fact un-American to create a law that implied that "those who come seeking opportunity are not to be admitted unless they have already had one of the chief opportunities they seek, the opportunity of education" (Wilson 69).

Though she believed immigrants had a right to education, Stewart did not accept the Americanizers' claims that most if not all immigrants were unschooled and illiterate. As a fanatical collector of statistics, Stewart emphasized in her speeches that native illiterates far outnumbered foreign-born illiterates and that Americanizers too often tended to blur the line between the ability to read and write and the ability to read and write *in English* (see, for example, "War Modified"). However, Stewart spent little time explicitly defending immigrants' educational attainments in public forums, in part because she felt she should instead call attention to native illiteracy—immigrant education had taken quite enough attention already. In spite of this reluctance, Stewart subtly attacked the idea that literacy had to be in English in order to "count" in three ways: first, by calling into question definitions and statistics associated with literacy education; second, by suggesting that Americanizers were engaged in something other than literacy education; and third, by emphasizing the non-English literacy skills of some Moonlight Schools students.

In her 1922 address to the National Council of Education (NCE), Stewart takes perhaps her most explicit public jab at the notion that "literacy" is equivalent to "literacy in English." Arguing that the role of the illiteracy committee of the NCE should be to function as a clearinghouse for literacy statistics, she opines that "the standards of literacy in this country are indefinite and variable" and points out, "Some define literacy as the inability to read, write, and speak the English language—a test which had it been adopted by France before President Wilson's visit to that country, would have put him in the illiterate class while there because he could not read, write, or speak its native tongue" ("Report of Committee" 455). For Stewart, literacy in any language brought the ability to distribute "rare talents" and knowledge, which, for her, were the essential benefits of literacy. In fact, Stewart promoted the Moonlight Schools at the World Conference on Education between 1923 and 1929, suggesting that the Moonlight Schools could be used to educate rural people in countries around the world. She even planned a trip to Russia to observe literacy conditions and, if possible, found Moonlight Schools.[11] Certainly, she envisioned no essential connection between the Moonlight Schools and English.

In the same address, Stewart writes scathingly of "illiteracy statistics varying so widely from fact [that they] will tend to convince the laymen that educators are very careless or not altogether informed" (456). Though not explicitly stated, Stewart is clearly pointing fingers at the Americanizers, as supporters of Americanization were the most prominent distributors of literacy statistics (other than Stewart herself).[12] In her letters, Stewart makes clear that she does not believe that Americanizers are "very careless or not altogether informed"—instead, she believes that they are interested in a continuing-education program focused on upper-level and university instruction for immigrants rather than the simple illiteracy and citizenship training courses they explicitly promoted ("Report of Committee" 456).

Her resistance to this larger program is most evident in her exchanges with Robert Deming, chairman of the NEA's Department of Adult Education. Stewart's NEA Illiteracy Committee offered its first report in 1918; the NEA's Department of Immigrant Education was formed in 1921. In 1925, the NEA joined these two agencies under Deming's leadership as the Department of Adult Education. Following the merger, Deming sent Stewart three letters expressing his enthusiasm for her work and inviting her to suggest ways that the Illiteracy Commission and the larger department could benefit one another. Stewart did not respond to either of the first two letters, pointedly ignoring Deming's request.[13] When she replied, five months after Deming's initial contact, she declined to undertake any shared work with the department, citing the differences between "adult education" and the "illiteracy crusade": "the friends of the illiteracy crusade, at least those who have been with it from the beginning, are unwilling to dissipate their energies in the various phases of adult education" (Stewart, Letter to Robert Deming, 14 Dec. 1925).

In a letter written on the same day to close friend A. E. Winship, Stewart is more explicit about the distinction she perceives between the work of "immigrant education" and literacy teachers:

> Some folk are about to confuse the issues. . . . The illiteracy
> crusade deals with all over ten years of age who cannot read
> or write. Since it takes in those in the teen age and tries to
> lead them into day schools, it could hardly be consistently
> called adult education. . . . I have made a hard fight to keep
> the illiteracy crusade from being confused with immigrant
> education and other things. We have a very definite
> proposition—it is simply to teach five million people to write
> and to do it in a given time. This opens up the way for them
> to go on through school and through college, and they will
> benefit by the adult education movement as much as others are
> now doing.

Stewart reiterates this distinction in another reply to Deming: "I am glad
that your Department is giving some time to illiteracy, though I realize that
you are covering a general field and cannot devote as much time to this one
problem as it deserves" (Stewart, Letter to Robert Deming, 22 Jan. 1926).
As Stewart explains to Winship, the adult education movement—which,
for Stewart, is essentially synonymous with immigrant education—does
not aim to teach those in need of basic literacy skills but rather those who
already have the rudiments of education. She compares the US adult
education movement to those in Europe, which target "educated men and
women" who would benefit from continued schooling (Letter to Robert
Deming, 14 Dec. 1925).

Clearly, Stewart is claiming that the Department of Immigrant Education is not concerned with issues of illiteracy.[14] Because Stewart largely
avoids discussing immigrant education programs (these exchanges between
Stewart and Deming and Stewart and Winship are the most voluminous
extant references to the issue), it is less certain what she believed was the
rationale for the department's focus on continuing education. However,
her pursuit of statistics concerning immigrant illiteracy and her conces-
sions to immigrant education in her textbooks suggest that she saw the
department as having tacitly recognized that many of the immigrants who
made up the student population for Americanization courses were, in fact,
literate and as having ignored literacy education in favor of more overtly
coercive methods of bringing immigrants in line with their conception of
"Americanness." These methods included the faulty equation of knowledge
of English with literacy.

Though her NCE speech is an exception, Stewart is rarely explicitly critical of the Americanizers' focus on English-language teaching; after all, the Moonlight Schools conducted schools in English. However, Stewart does take advantage of opportunities to emphasize the non-English literacy abilities of Moonlight Schools students. For instance, in *Moonlight Schools: For the Emancipation of Adult Illiterates*, Stewart recognizes the Spanish literacy abilities some students possessed: "This county [Santa Fé County, New Mexico] had a large Mexican population, some of whom could read and write in Spanish, but came to the moonlight schools to learn to read and write in English" (132). In Moonlight Schools work the Bureau of Indian Affairs conducted, teachers documented students' language and literacy abilities in *all* languages, not only English, resulting in an impressive recognition of the cultural diversity within (as well as among) reservations. And, in promoting the Moonlight Schools globally, Stewart indicates her belief that pedagogy is—and should be—separable from its language of instruction.

The Cost

Perhaps the best evidence of Stewart's disdain for Americanization programs is her refusal to join forces with any Americanization groups. This decision cost Stewart, both figuratively and literally. We can read Stewart's acceptance of these costs in several ways: as a testament to her conviction that literacy was essential and that all people should have equal rights to an education that guarantees literacy; as an indication of her zealous belief in the superiority of her own methods; or, perhaps most generously, as reflective of her belief that the Americanization movement was unrealistic, unpatriotic, and unethical.

The literal costs that Stewart absorbed for her refusal to join the Americanization movement nearly bankrupted her. The rural states that most needed Moonlight Schools (and that began statewide initiatives to organize them) were the states least willing or able to fund schools for adults. Given her work as a superintendent, Stewart was well versed in these funding problems. Though she adamantly believed that the Moonlight Schools were a positive investment for the state—the inefficiency, unemployment, and crime caused by illiteracy would, she argued, be eliminated if the Moonlight Schools were properly funded—she found it difficult to argue against school superintendents who insisted that the little educational money available would be better spent on teacher salaries. Stewart was forced to rely solely on donations from private sources to fund literacy efforts across the country. When these funds ran out, Stewart spent her own money to continue the work. In Kentucky, "Stewart often financed the work of the [Kentucky Illiteracy] commission 'from her own pocket'" (Baldwin 76) while also lamenting that she "cannot pay [her] own personal debts" (Stewart, Letter to Lela Mae Stiles).

In contrast, Americanizers were well funded from a variety of public sources. Private donors, too, were more forthcoming in providing funds for Americanization than for Moonlight Schools. The NEA's funding of the Illiteracy Commission and the Department of Immigrant Education reflects the trend of funding for the two movements. The Illiteracy Commission was funded by NEA grants that covered Stewart's expenses (and it is worth noting that these checks rarely arrived on time) (Baldwin 141, 144). This relationship required Stewart to constantly justify both the work of the commission and her own use of NEA funds. Though the Department of Immigrant Education also received money directly from the NEA, it also "had a membership, collected dues, elected officers and boards of directors" (Luke 10)—that is, it functioned as an autonomous unit that dispersed its funds (gained from membership dues and donations) as it saw fit. In nearly every encounter with potential donors, Stewart had both to document the need for Moonlight Schools and to demonstrate their success; nearly all of her public speeches include invocations of specific students who have learned to read and write and offer to display letters written by these students. The need and efficacy of Americanization programs, conversely, were taken as givens by most state and municipal governments, factory owners, and private donors—despite near unanimous agreement among researchers who studied Americanization programs that the classes were totally ineffective in teaching either spoken or written English (see, for example, Miller).

Had Stewart chosen to reframe her work as a variety of Americanization, much more funding would have been available to her—even if native illiteracy remained her primary concern, she could have used income generated by her affiliation with Americanizers to fund rural Moonlight Schools. Refusing to join forces with Deming or other Americanization advocates meant sacrificing these funding opportunities and, by extension, meant innumerable hours spent campaigning for more money. To borrow, for a moment, Stewart's hyperbolic rhetoric, her decision likely also cost thousands of native illiterates the opportunity for more schoolbooks, better schoolhouses, and longer Moonlight Schools terms.

Money was not the only sacrifice Stewart made in forgoing calls to become an Americanizer: because almost all other adult educators of the period were involved with Americanization, Stewart was marginalized professionally by her decision to focus exclusively on native illiteracy. For example, when the NCE finally agreed to Stewart's call to form a Committee on Adult Illiteracy in 1921, the committee was made up of "seven state superintendents of education, one former state superintendent, two newspaper editors, and two adult education practitioners [one of whom was Stewart]," instead of "a group of literacy experts" as Stewart had asked (Luke 56). These experts, Luke explains, were not appointed because they were occupied with duties elsewhere—duties with the Committee on Instruction of Immigrants and the Interstate Council on Immigrant Education, organizations focused solely on the education of immigrant populations, particularly adult immigrants. Stewart eventually cut many ties with both the NEA and the General Federation of Women's Clubs because during the organization of the first National Illiteracy Conference—an event Stewart both created and planned but the NEA, GFWC, and the Bureau of Education sponsored —Stewart was pushed aside by the commissioner of the Bureau of Education, James Tigert, as well as the educators who represented the GFWC on the grounds that the event she had organized did not include enough nationally known educators (that is, more Americanization advocates) (Baldwin 151–52).

Though both Stewart and the Americanizers had faded from national prominence by 1935, Stewart's refusal to merge with the Americanizers has been one source of her historical marginalization. As argued elsewhere, the Moonlight Schools influenced (and continue to influence) current conditions in the field of literacy education in two ways: by (re)defining the importance of literacy and (re)creating literacy as a public issue and by spawning debate about who had the ability to teach reading and writing. As the Moonlight Schools' counterpoint, Americanization courses also contributed to this dialogue, and, in fact, the Americanizers' vision of who should teach reading and writing has become accepted policy in most organized literacy programs. Stewart's refusal to participate in the conversation surrounding Americanization led to her marginalization among literacy professionals, which undercut any future for a volunteer model of literacy teaching within an increasingly professionalized society. However, Stewart's refusal to participate in Americanization is also perhaps the best reason for modern scholars to recover her important work.

5. PROFESSIONALIZING ADULT EDUCATION

*B*etween 1910 and 1930, the *Addresses and Proceedings* of the NEA's annual meetings document increasing awareness of and concern for the education of illiterates. However, the overwhelming focus of attention during this period was not who should be taught or what they should learn but, rather, *who should teach*. This question occupied the time of nearly every NEA department and committee, from elementary through higher education. Of course, any discussion of illiteracy or its associated issues—compulsory education, rural school funding, Americanization— necessarily addressed this question. If the goal was to find the cause of illiteracy, educators asked why adequate teaching was not present; if the goal was to find the solution, educators asked who would teach the millions of illiterates (and/or immigrants). Today, education is seen as the work of professionals—one cannot teach in a public school without credentials from a higher education program, and rhetoric and composition programs exist in part to provide appropriate credentials for teachers of advanced literacy practices—yet nearly all adult education programs, including both Americanization and the Moonlight Schools, began as volunteer efforts. This chapter begins by considering the state and status of elementary education as the primary site of literacy education in the first decade of the twentieth century; specifically, the chapter examines the tension between efforts to professionalize teachers and efforts to find adequate numbers of teachers to staff rural schools. Then explored are the literacy education efforts of the Moonlight Schools and Americanization as two widely disparate reactions to this tension between professionalization and material conditions. Finally, the chapter details how attitudes toward volunteer teaching changed—

and were changed by—the interaction between Moonlight Schools advocates and Americanizers.

Background

Though local-level discussions concerning who should teach have existed since the first European settlements of the United States, the question became a national issue when common school education became increasingly widespread in the 1830s and 1840s. In particular, the high volume of common schools in rural areas demanded a rurally based teaching corps. For instance, as late as 1906, Kentucky had over eight thousand school districts, all requiring at least one teacher (Kett 319). Two problems arose in attempts to fill this demand: comparatively few rural people had attained high levels of education prior to the formation of the common schools, and those who had attained such education sought careers in more prestigious and better-compensated fields. As a result, during the early decades of the common school movement, rural schools were most often taught by temporary teachers who worked only during winter months and who were attempting to earn money to finance their own education in other, more lucrative fields (Herbst 22). In the latter half of the nineteenth century, women increasingly filled positions as common schoolteachers, but women often saw teaching as temporary employment until marriage, not as a permanent vocation. As might be expected, the quality of teaching was often poor, and replacing teachers was often a never-ending process for local school boards.

In response to the problem of supplying rural teachers, R. Freeman Butts and Lawrence Cremin explain, educational advocates argued as early as 1835 that "high standards would not be met, nor permanent, professional teachers secured until salaries were increased to the point where competent persons could be attained and held in teaching" (231–32). In addition, these educators—including common school theorist Horace Mann—argued that the states should fund training schools to prepare elementary school teachers for their work. In response to these calls, public normal schools were first founded in Massachusetts in 1839 and were initially focused on providing instruction for elementary educators.

Many legislators, though, disagreed with the idea that a normal school education was necessary for future teachers and opposed this expenditure of state funds. For instance, the Massachusetts House Committee on

Education argued "that every person, who has himself undergone a process of instruction, must acquire, by that very process, the art of instructing others" (Dodge 183). As educational historian Jurgen Herbst explains, in the logic of the committee, "From this it followed that normal schools were superfluous" (64). Their position was bolstered by the failure of the normal schools to produce trained teachers. Normal schools were caught in a vicious cycle of remedial education: because schooling conditions—including both teaching and material conditions—were so poor, normal school students often entered their training coursework with little background education; before the normal schools could offer instruction on teaching, they first had to teach students the basic subject matter that they would be required to impart to their future pupils. This left little time for lessons in pedagogy. In light of these difficulties, Herbst argues that the Massachusetts schools "had not solved the rural school crisis" (86).

Despite the failure of the Massachusetts normal schools to provide adequate numbers of trained teachers, state-supported normal schools spread throughout the country during the nineteenth century. However, the focus of these schools moved increasingly toward preparation for high school teachers and administrators. Educators recognized that "as long as America's rural schools were governed by local boards and their teachers were subject to lay direction in professional matters, neither could rural teachers regard themselves as professionals nor would they serve in any other capacity than as temporary shopkeepers" (Herbst 102). One way to increase the prestige of the profession and frame its members as professionals was to focus on advanced courses rather than elementary education—that is, education that not just anyone could provide (Herbst 187–88). Elementary teacher training was relegated to "high school normal classes, to county or city training schools, and to the undergraduate departments of teachers colleges and state universities"—none of which were easily accessible to the rural women who filled the majority of elementary teaching posts (Herbst 188). As a result of both the realignment of normal schools to favor high school teacher training and the widespread conception that any educated person could teach, few rural teachers pursued any form of advanced education; an 1887 Bureau of Education report found that fewer than 10 percent of the 225,000 teachers in the United States had attended a normal school (Kett 164).

Even this low percentage, however, overestimates the training of US teachers. Many of those who attended normal schools failed to complete the entire course (Butts and Cremin 449); because the Bureau of Education surveyed attendance, rather than completion, its figures should not be interpreted as representing the number of teachers who underwent a full training program. Furthermore, a normal school certificate was no guarantee of a quality education. Many normal schools themselves suffered from poor teaching, and the course offerings were "confined largely to the methods and mechanics of the classroom" (Cremin 169) and taught "almost entirely on the secondary level" (Butts and Cremin 449).

The low availability of, low quality of, and little necessity for teacher training in the nineteenth century meant that most students were taught by teachers whose qualifications were simply the ability to read, write, cipher, and remember key historical dates. Often the only requirement one needed to meet in order to teach a common school was to have graduated from that common school. As inconceivable as it may seem today, throughout the nineteenth and early twentieth centuries, the overwhelming majority of people who learned to read and write were taught at home, at school, or at church by women and men who had no teaching qualifications whatsoever.

University Involvement

Though higher education did not begin to provide a route to professionalization for elementary school teachers until the 1930s, between 1890 and 1920, universities became increasingly invested in education as a field of study. Normal schools also "began to design regular four-year baccalaureate courses, thereby converting themselves into collegiate institutions" while continuing to frame their work as the training of teachers (Cremin 169). The most well-known and influential institution of higher learning for teachers during the period was Teachers College, affiliated with Columbia University. Its program of instruction included three areas of "professional knowledge" that were adapted by many other education programs: "educational psychology and child study," "history of education and comparative education," and "school administration and its relation to the teacher, student, and society" (Cremin 174). However, Teachers College and other institutions served primarily as "colleges for the teachers of teachers" (Herbst 105). After having invested both time and, in many cases, money to pursue a degree in education, few graduates of teachers' colleges aimed to return to the low status, poorly paid work of elementary schools.

In fact, the development of teachers' colleges in many ways further diminished the status of elementary school teachers, especially in rural areas. As Herbst explains in regard to the Massachusetts normal schools, institutes offering teacher education "aided—unwittingly, to be sure—what we have come to call the brain drain from the country" (84); those rural men and women who sought normal school education rarely "stayed or returned to play the role of country schoolmaster or schoolmistress" (84). Most normal schools and teachers' colleges had, by 1900, required applicants to have completed high school—thus, the rural attendees often represented the most qualified potential teachers in their home area. Only those who could not qualify for admission or those who had no desire to attend (suggesting, perhaps, a lack of interest in teaching as a permanent career) were left to fill rural school posts.

More important, the creation of a body of professional educational theorists resulted in a divide between those who practiced teaching and those who were recognized as authorities on teaching practice. This split is evident in the *Addresses and Proceedings* of the NEA's annual conferences. Between 1907 and 1915, only three (or 6 percent) of fifty speakers to the Department of Kindergarten Education were identified as kindergarten teachers.[1] In the same period, the Department of Elementary Education featured no speakers identified as elementary school teachers. Instead, speakers were drawn overwhelmingly from the ranks of teachers' college and normal school professors and superintendents of education.[2] In its choice of speakers, the NEA—by far the most influential collection of educators of the period (and today)—implied that elementary school teachers were not able to contribute to the theory of elementary education.

Judging by the increasingly fervent calls from speakers in the Department of Rural Education that the solution to the "rural school problem" must begin with giving teachers incentive to engage in professional development, elementary educators, for their part, largely ignored the rhetoric and pedagogical suggestions put forward by educational theorists. Certainly, much of the resistance to these pedagogies was not resistance at all but, rather, a predictable result of the temporary status of elementary teachers—some were likely not even aware of the growing body of literature on educational practices. In other areas, though, school boards and superintendents pushed teachers to engage in professional development; many required teachers to attend a summer training institute to maintain their posts, while others—including Cora Wilson Stewart—required their teachers to subscribe to educationally focused publications. But even where teachers had access to educational theory and were invested in implementing new pedagogies, material conditions of schooling often prevented meaningful change. For example, during the 1910 annual meeting of the Department of Elementary Education, one speaker argued that elementary geography should "be taught to interpret the history of a country and the chief occupations of its people from studying a good map of that part of the earth's surface" (Greenwood 437). Though elementary educators then and now could recognize the value of this suggestion, not all rural schools were equipped with sources of heat or adequate desks—maps were an even less frequent luxury.

The division between theorists and rural practitioners was nowhere more evident than in discussions surrounding literacy education. As NEA speaker Adelaide Steele Baker explained in 1910:

> No subject, in recent years, has received more attention at the hands of the teaching force than English. Over a decade ago, more than a dozen national and sectional conferences had been held to repair the gross evils in the teaching of English, while general and local organizations, clubs, and committees have continued to put forth untiring efforts to investigate and improve the work. . . . The qualifications of elementary-school teachers have been based upon their extensive preparations in the subject of English, a criterion that has led to the special pride taken by normal schools and higher institutions of learning in their extensive English courses. (430)

Baker is quoted at length because her speech illustrates two recurring themes in discussions of elementary English education: first, among those who are said to have investigated and improved the work, no teachers are mentioned;[3] second, elementary school teachers are assumed to have been extensively prepared for their work, and school boards are assumed to care whether or not the teachers have been prepared. Though most teachers were required to undergo some variety of certification, many certification exams tested knowledge of basic common school curriculum—no advanced or "extensive" work was required to pass. The English qualifications of many teachers extended no further than the English lessons available in local high schools. While English education became a central area of study in higher institutions, it remained the province of teachers whose qualifications were those the Massachusetts House Committee on Education outlined in 1840: because teachers could read and write, they possessed the necessary qualifications to teach others to read and write.

Who Teaches Moonlight Schools?

Before any Moonlight Schools sessions could be held, Stewart had to answer the same question that had plagued school organizers for nearly one hundred years: who should—or who would—teach? Her answer was similar to the Massachusetts House Committee, though Stewart took a two-pronged approach. All literate people could and should offer immediate instruction to illiterates, working to move them from absolute illiteracy toward a familiarity with the basics of reading and writing. In the long term, volunteer, day school teachers trained to instruct adult students were the best option to move students toward their fullest potential. For the initial meeting of the Moonlight Schools, Rowan County elementary school teachers were "asked to volunteer" (*Moonlight Schools: . . . Illiterates* 14).[4] From the outset, then, the Moonlight Schools participated in an economic devaluation of elementary teaching: men and women were expected to double their workload but were given no extra salary or benefits.

But the effects of the Moonlight Schools on the status of elementary teachers were nuanced and multiple. In spite of the economic devaluation of teachers' time and effort, the Moonlight Schools also led to an increased respect for local educators as individuals. The adults who attended the Moonlight Schools had previously had little cause or opportunity to interact with the day school teachers. Some saw education as an unnecessary luxury; others were ashamed of their illiteracy. The Moonlight Schools classes presented an opportunity for these adults to work closely with the teachers and to see the teachers as volunteers who both respected their habits and beliefs and sought to improve their lives. Many of the personal letters Moonlight Schools students sent to Stewart mention the work of local teachers, and specific teachers are often singled out by name. James Smith writes that "Miss Audrey Chapman is [his] teacher" (*Moonlight Schools: . . . Illiterates* 81); Amanda McElroy thanks Stewart and "our Carrollton teachers" (83) for their good work.[5] Students who learned to read and write during the sessions could have little cause to doubt the abilities of their local teachers or the efficacy of their methods for teaching literacy. While teaching's status as a profession was economically devalued by the Moonlight Schools, the status of the schools as institutes of learning and the teachers as purveyors of knowledge were increased, at least at a local level.

As the Moonlight Schools grew, Stewart encouraged others to take on the role of teacher. In the third Rowan County session, every person who had the ability to read and write was encouraged to find someone to instruct. Though we can read Stewart's claims as hyperbolic, her assertion that "doctors were soon teaching their convalescent patients, ministers were teaching members of their flocks, children were teaching their parents, stenographers were teaching waitresses in the small town hotels, and the person in the county without a pupil was considered a very useless sort of individual" does indicate that Stewart and other Moonlight Schools supporters believed in the adage that anyone who had attended school could be a teacher (*Moonlight Schools: . . . Illiterates* 48). In particular, Stewart cites former Moonlight Schools students who "became itinerant teachers, going from district to district giving lessons" (*Moonlight Schools: . . . Illiterates* 48). "They were successful teachers," she states, because "they attempted to give lessons in reading and writing only. . . . Their visits to illiterate homes started the process of learning in most cases, and cleared the way for the teacher who was to follow with more complete and thorough knowledge" (*Moonlight Schools: . . . Illiterates* 49). The Moonlight Schools' philosophy, then, held that anyone could teach a subject in which they had been instructed—no specialized knowledge of either the subject or of the art of teaching was necessary.

However, if anyone could teach, it was still true that not all teachers were created equal. Trained elementary school teachers, with their "more complete and thorough knowledge" of both teaching and the basic curriculum of the Moonlight Schools, were portrayed as the most able Moonlight Schools instructors. Stewart also believed that specialized knowledge about educating adults would make Moonlight Schools volunteers better teachers. To train teachers for Moonlight Schools' work, Stewart held Moonlight Schools' institutes, which offered discussion in "the methods of teaching adult illiterates, materials to use, ways and means of reaching the stubborn and getting them into school and other things relative to the problem of educating adults" (*Moonlight Schools: . . . Illiterates* 32). She also published her guidebooks *Moonlight Schools* to provide teachers with "inspiration and guidance" for organizing and teaching schools (vii). Yet, Stewart adds that the text is "purposely written in simple language and kept free from technical terms. It is . . . as easy and accessible to those who have had little preparation for teaching as to those who are experienced and trained" (viii), reaffirming that the Moonlight Schools could be taught by any educated person, regardless of their training in teaching. It is also worth noting that teachers not only had to volunteer their time to the Moonlight Schools' institute but they also had to "pay their own expenses," including travel and lodging, while present (32). Once again, while Moonlight Schools economically devalued teachers' time and effort, the schools also celebrated the teachers' professional qualifications.

As the Moonlight Schools were expanded through Stewart's work with the Kentucky Illiteracy Commission (KIC), the voluntary teaching model became even more important. The KIC initially had no funds with which to employ teachers; when funds were at last appropriated, they were far too few to adequately support the teaching staff needed for the schools. Stewart continued to advocate that any educated person could and should take on the work of teaching illiterates, but she focused much of her rhetoric on elementary school teachers because she felt that teachers were best equipped to instruct illiterates, and elementary school teachers composed by far the largest body of teachers in Kentucky (and the United States). Although there is no evidence that Stewart recognized in her initial planning that one effect of teachers volunteering for work in the Moonlight Schools would be an increased respect for the teacher (though she certainly recognized that the schools would produce an increased respect for education as an institution), she capitalized on this appeal in her public addresses during her work with the KIC. In particular, during World War I, Stewart pointed to the Moonlight Schools as a way for teachers to demonstrate their patriotism. Their willingness to teach, she comments, is a "test [of their] patriotism and devotion to education" ("Call"). It was not only a "duty" but a "high privilege" to educate illiterate soldiers before they were deployed to France. Perhaps recognizing that her emphasis on volunteer teaching could be seen as an economic devaluation of teachers' work, Stewart also includes an economic appeal: "We may have been unable to invest in Liberty Loan Bonds. It may not be ours to follow the boys to France to minister to them under the Red Cross, but we can add to their comfort their self-respect and efficiency by giving them this [literacy] training before they go" ("Call"). By equating literacy teaching with more tangible physical donations of time and money, Stewart gives teachers a way to understand themselves as contributing fully to the war effort without having to sacrifice either their meager paychecks or their teaching positions. Though this appeal likely had little effect beyond its audience of teachers—it did not help improve the teachers' public status—Stewart does encourage teachers to place higher value on their own work.

The Moonlight Schools remained a volunteer-based effort until their demise in the early 1930s. But Stewart's public rationale for a volunteer teaching force became increasingly nuanced as she found herself competing with Americanizers for public attention and financing. The Americanizers' far different answer to the question of who should teach became the key battleground between the two movements, and the debate between the two shaped the public discourse surrounding literacy education.

Who Teaches Americanization?

The Americanization movement rejected the idea that "anyone" could be qualified to teach literacy, English speaking, or civics. Michael R. Olneck argues that Americanization was symbolically important because it "assigned to native-born Americans the roles of tutor, interpreter, and gatekeeper, while rendering immigrants the subjects of tutelage and judgment" (416). If any English speaker were qualified to teach, there would be no need for native-born teachers; immigrants who had already learned English could pass this knowledge on to new arrivals. The Americanizers' call for specialization highlighted the idea that the knowledge teachers possessed was different and better—in every sense of the word—than the knowledge immigrants possessed, even if those immigrants had been educated in their native country. Also, because the Americanizers linked education with American identity, those with more education—that is, professional educators—were imagined as the "most" American and, as such, the most apt teachers for immigrant students.[6] Instead, Americanizers pushed for the professionalization of adult education. I draw on Burton Bledstein to define "professionalization" as a

> fairly difficult and time-consuming process [by which] a person mastered an esoteric but useful body of systematic knowledge, completed theoretical training before entering a practice or apprenticeship, and received a degree or license from a recognized institution. A professional person in the role of a practitioner insisted upon technical competence, superior skill, and a high quality of performance. (86–87)

In the case of Americanizers, professionalization involved teacher training courses specializing in the theory of adult education, as well as a general expectation that all teachers should be graduates of some higher learning institution (at least a normal school, if not a college or university).

However, it would be inaccurate to suggest that Americanizers never employed volunteers; the Americanization "movement" was ultimately a nebulous and loosely defined grouping of public and private organizations and courses. Just as volunteers were inspired by the rhetoric of the Moonlight Schools, many more were inspired by the appeals to patriotism and national defense Americanizers made. In the Bureau of Education's manual *Training Teachers for Americanization*, Fred Butler refers to the "hundreds of volunteers [that] have taken up the work throughout the country . . . as a patriotic duty" (6). In spite of this reliance on volunteers, the rhetoric of the movement emphasized the need for its teachers to have professional training not only in teaching but also in the specific field of adult education. Butler's attention to volunteers is not to applaud their willingness to donate their time but, rather, to suggest *Training Teachers* as a remedy for the fact that these volunteers "have not had the opportunity of studying their subject" (6). He also emphasizes that the text itself is not produced by teachers or volunteers but by a "committee of leading experts in this field of education" (6).

Though the importance of trained teachers was a key component of Americanization rhetoric throughout the first two decades of the twentieth century—in his 1906 study, Huebner emphasizes the superior resources of trained day school teachers for Americanizing children—Americanization remained the province of volunteers until the 1920s. McClymer explains that "few school systems had, prior to 1916, ongoing programs for adult education," and there were correspondingly few "proven techniques [or] tested curricula available to the thousands of school systems that hurriedly inaugurated Americanization classes" ("Americanization" 105) after US entrance into World War I. In 1919, P. P. Claxton, the commissioner of education, declared that "we have had very little experience, and there are few established and accepted principles or methods of procedure" for teaching adult immigrants (5).

Even if pedagogical methods had been studied, there were few organized efforts to train teachers for Americanization work. A 1919 study found that the total number of teachers in sixty-one representative cities engaged in Americanization work was 592, and of these 207 have had professional training of and also special training in Americanization work. . . . [O]f these 207, 157 were in four cities out of the sixty-one. Thus fifty-seven cities reported only fifty public school teachers with special training for the work. (R. Gray 224)

At a 1919 Americanization conference, W. C. Smith reminds his audience that "it is within the short memory of everyone of us here that there was any definite method taken for the training of teachers in this great work" (108). That Smith was attending an Americanization conference, though, indicates the increasing organization of the Americanization movement. As the raison d'être for Americanization classes waned with the end of the war and the imposition of more stringent immigration requirements (including a literacy test), the movement needed to appeal to more than patriotic fervor and nativist fear to continue its mission. Though Americanizers' emphasis on "creating citizens" remained strong, the rhetoric of the movement increasingly invoked the specialized knowledge of its teachers and leadership as the feature that separated Americanization efforts from other mass education movements—including the Moonlight Schools.

Just as the Moonlight Schools' emphasis on volunteer teaching arose from both deep-seated belief and the pressures of material conditions, so did the Americanizers' push for professionalization. As the Bureau of Education's teacher-training manual makes clear, many Americanization courses simply were not effective. As its primary author, John J. Mahoney, explains, "The schooling of the immigrant in the past has been, speaking broadly, an unsuccessful endeavor" (7). The Carnegie Corporation's study of Americanization finds that "there is not only . . . relative failure to enroll in evening classes, but . . . [a] disconcerting lack of persistency of attendance. The more efficient evening schools hold their students better than the less efficient, but not much better" (Thompson 95). The study also asserts that "the evening school by its nature cannot be an institution completely adapted to the needs of immigrants, and conversely, that the majority of immigrants find it impossible to use the evening school as their means of education" (98), because immigrants could not do the work the evening schools required in addition to their often-arduous factory work, night shifts, or family conditions.

However, few Americanizers were willing to accept that their programs would not be fully effective. While pedagogical methods, school facilities, and immigrants themselves were often blamed for the failure of the evening schools to find and retain students, the majority of this failure was attributed to the lack of teacher training. Mahoney, for instance, asserts, "One of the principle reasons, without a doubt, [for the lack of success,] was the slowness on the part of the public and not infrequently on the part of school people themselves, to appreciate the fact that the teaching of the adult immigrant is a highly specialized piece of work, requiring not only special aptitude but special training as well" (7).[7] Frank V. Thompson, in the Carnegie Corporation report, asserts that "looming large among those causes [of the failure of the evening schools]" was that "for years the evening school was but an appendage of the educational system, and for years it was felt that anyone could teach an evening school class" (262). But as Herbert Miller points out in his critique of the quality of teaching in evening schools, "There seems to be no effective supervision, no plan for improving the teachers in service, and no effort to find out which of the many methods used produces the best results" (94). Even the most vociferous critics of evening school teaching acknowledged that the lack of teacher training was not the fault of the teachers. Unlike day school teachers who, many felt, had adequate access to training opportunities, few cities offered even one-day courses in adult education methods. Teacher-training programs were thus framed as an essential requirement for the continued existence of Americanization programs.

Most Americanizers argued that normal schools and universities were the best option for training teachers in adult education because these schools could provide lengthy courses. Emory Stephen Bogardus, for instance, suggests that normal school courses should offer "training in field work," which "should include at least three hours a week of practice teaching of adults for several months under careful supervision" (291). Robert Floyd Gray goes further, suggesting that while normal schools must offer courses that include "observation and practise [sic]," in addition, "the state department should organize teachers' institutes to aid teachers already in service" (227). In both types of training courses, the material covered should include "a background of our various immigrant peoples," "the meanings and interpretations of Americanism," "the teaching of English to both beginners and advanced students," "industrial Americanization," "Americanization of women," and "field work" and should develop a "sympathetic attitude toward the alien" (R. Gray 229). To cover this volume of material, lengthy courses taught by specialized teachers were necessary.

Other Americanizers recognized that the transition from an untrained and often volunteer teaching corps to a trained, paid group of educators would need to happen gradually if Americanization courses were to continue unabated. YMCA organizer Peter Roberts, for instance, agrees with his contemporaries that Americanization workers should attend "a normal class" (206), but his demands were less strenuous: the course would meet "at least every other week" (206), and volunteers would be permitted to specify the work for which they felt they were most suited, rather than attempting to learn the entirety of the (little) accumulated knowledge about adult education methods. The recommendations of the Oakland (California) Department of Americanization for 1918–19 includes the suggestion that night school teachers be required to attend a training course only one afternoon of each week, and teachers were permitted to continue teaching as they completed the course (United States Cong. 106).

Nearly all Americanizers agreed, though, that teachers had to be paid for their work. As Roberts, the least militant advocate of professionalization among Americanization's leading organizers, warns, "When volunteers are sought, it should be clearly stated what is expected of them. If they are to teach for two nights a week, let it be clearly understood that the work will continue for three or four months and not interminably" (206–7). Roberts's concern was that teachers were likely to lose interest in teaching the lengthy courses Americanizers preferred if they were not paid for their work—hence the comfort to volunteers that their work would not go on forever. Others pointed out that teachers would not undergo training if there was no tangible reward: "if this work requires a specialized form of training and service the financial return must be adequate to the outlay of time and expense for the training" (W. Smith 109). Also, the most "gifted" teachers would not enter the field if pay were not sufficient (W. Smith 109). If Americanization teachers were paid the same amount of money as other elementary teachers, there would be no motivation for them to train beyond the standard normal school preparation for elementary school work. In order to justify higher pay, Americanizers had to posit that their teachers were undertaking work far more complex than that of elementary teachers, work that *could not* be done by just "anyone."

Moving Beyond Americanization

By 1925, the Americanization movement had begun to fade. The stringent immigration laws enacted in 1917 and 1921 decreased the flood of immigrants to a trickle, and the patriotic fervor of the war and anti-Bolshevik hysteria of the postwar years could not be maintained during the relative prosperity of the 1920s. But the combined efforts of Americanization and the Moonlight Schools had awakened American politicians and educators to the fact that adults were apt students, while the army tests administered to drafted men demonstrated that a much-higher percentage of adults, foreign and native, were in need of instruction in both basic and advanced topics than had previously been recognized. Moreover, the Americanization movement, with its push for training and specialization, had created a body of trained teachers and a plethora of training programs. The question that now faced the men and women who had led the Americanization movement was what should be done with the infrastructure their professionalization efforts created.

Their answer was adult education. Moving away from their narrow focus on educating immigrants, educators broadened their work to include all facets of adult education, particularly "continuing" education that focused on advanced skills needed for college preparation. This reframing allowed former Americanization trainees to keep their claim to unique specialization—they were the only educators trained to teach pre-college-level adults. Many adult education–related programs and agencies existed between 1925 and 1930, but three were notable for shaping public and field-specific discourse about the methods and, more important, the definition of adult education: the Office of Education, the American Association for Adult Education (AAAE), and the NEA's Department of Adult Education.

Of these, the US government's Office of Education was both the most symbolically important and the least effective of the agencies in addressing adult education. Until the mid-1950s, the Office of Education's involvement in adult education was directed by the principal specialist in adult education, appointed by the commissioner of education. Malcolm Knowles explains that the specialist "was accorded relatively low status" (101) within the office. During the 1920s and 1930s, the specialist was variously attached to the secondary education division, an adult education section, and the New Deal Emergency Education Program, suggesting that the role of adult education was ill-defined and considered nebulous in relation to the primary work of the office (Grattan 251; Knowles 101). The limited influence of the specialist is notable in reference to my study for two reasons. First, the appointment of the specialist signaled governmental recognition and approval of efforts to educate adults and signified in its very name that *specialization* in the field could and did exist, lending moral if not material support to efforts to professionalize adult education work. However, it is also significant that as the position was originally imagined, qualifications were based on experience rather than educational attainment. Stewart was, in fact, offered the position of specialist by Claxton in 1917 (she declined because she felt that she had a responsibility to finish out her work in Kentucky) (Baldwin 107). Secondly, although the specialist was given little authority to initiate programs or research relating to adult education, s/he could provide resources (primarily manpower and material resources rather than monetary assistance) to both the NEA and the AAAE; much of the work done by these two more visible groups would not have been as easily achieved without the assistance given by the Office of Education.

The AAAE, founded in 1926, required far less assistance than the NEA. Supported by the Carnegie Corporation, the AAAE had little need to seek out external funding; the corporation distributed "just under $3,000,000" in grants to "organizations that engaged in adult education" between 1924 and 1934 (Kett 334). The AAAE described itself as "a 'clearinghouse' for ideas and as a consultant to the corporation" concerning the distribution of these grants (Kett 334), and it functioned primarily as a research entity whose main purpose was to "interpret, explain, and to clarify, and only in a limited degree to propagandize for adult education" (qtd. in Knowles 195). Perhaps more important, the AAAE published the *Journal of Adult Education,* which remained the leading publication in the field until the journal's closure in 1941. As Kett explains, the AAAE and Carnegie Corporation "assisted the publication of more than a score of important studies on topics ranging from university extension to libraries and correspondence schools, the use of leisure and the habits of readers, community drama and parent education" (334). Though the Carnegie Corporation demonstrated far more interest (and contributed far more money) toward the education of immigrants than native illiteracy and though the impetus for the formation of the AAAE was the Carnegie-sponsored study *Schooling of the Immigrant,* the AAAE, unlike the Department of Adult Education, did contribute to the development of programs for native illiterate. In fact, beginning in

1931, Cora Wilson Stewart pursued the AAAE as a source of funding for her illiteracy crusade.[8]

As this list suggests, the AAAE's most significant contribution to the discourse surrounding adult education was to link the work of Americanizers and the Moonlight Schools to a far broader conception of "adult education." For the AAAE, "adult education" became synonymous with "educating adults"—any program that taught any adult a skill, even if that skill was a leisure activity, was considered "adult education." In fact, the AAAE declared that it would "resist all pressures for 'the formation of a final and somewhat rigid definition of adult education' by which certain adult activities partially of an educational nature would be excluded from the field" (Knowles 195). This expanded definition appealed to Americanizers whose role in basic literacy education was (perceived to be) no longer necessary. Yet, even if immigrants possessed the rudiments of education, there was still much to teach, and an expanded definition of adult education helped describe and, by extension, support this work.

The AAAE was also instrumental in professionalizing the field of adult education. In addition to financially supporting existing teacher-training courses at Teachers College, the AAAE later asked the Carnegie Corporation to create "twelve fellowships in adult education" at the school and to donate funds to pay for the "appointment to full professorship on the Teachers College faculty . . . a specially qualified person who could devote himself to the further development and critical evaluation of the adult education teacher training experiment" (American 24). The AAAE also supported training efforts at other colleges, including "Yale, the Hudson Shore Labor School, Claremont College, and New York University" (Knowles 208). The makeup of the leadership and membership of the AAAE also reflected this emphasis on professionalization; their members were to be those who "have a direct and usually a *professional* interest in adult education" (AAAE qtd. in Knowles 197; emphasis added). Furthermore, the AAAE's leadership was selected by the Carnegie Corporation from among well-known educators; as Knowles emphasizes, "the practitioners in general, and the public school practitioners in particular—the most numerous single group in the field,—were underrepresented" among the leadership of the AAAE (192; see also Luke 96–97).

Though the AAAE's lack of representation for teachers seems egregious, we can read this omission as made in deference to the NEA's Department of Adult Education. The department's membership was "limited to workers in the public schools and its purpose was to serve their individual needs" (Knowles 210); though these "workers" were most often superintendents and other administrators rather than teachers, most did deal directly with questions of pedagogy and enrollment. The AAAE, conversely, sought to include the voices of adult education "professionals" who were not public school practitioners, professionals who worked to theorize the field of adult education but who engaged in little hands-on work with students. In design, the two organizations were complementary; the department's president, Charles Herlihy, was present during the meeting of adult educators that gave birth to the AAAE, tacitly demonstrating the department's support of the AAAE's aims (Luke 94).

This supportive relationship did not last. In 1927, the department's definition of membership broadened. In its "Report of the Commission on Coordination in Adult Education," the department defines "adult education" as education occurring under "public auspices" rather than "in public schools" (Alderman et al. 328). This definition broadened the department's work and membership to include "facilities for foreign-born and native-born of all degrees of educational attainment, in schools of elementary, secondary and higher grade, vocational and technical schools, normal schools, colleges, and universities" as well as "libraries, art galleries, and museums" (327, 328). Though the department does make a gesture at avoiding overlap with the AAAE—the report specifies that "education of any grade and character, under corporate or private auspices or for profit, is not included" in its definition of adult education (327)—this redefinition of "public" placed the department squarely in conflict with the AAAE, both for members (Knowles suggests that by 1951, half of the groups' memberships overlapped) and for influence and professional authority (Knowles 212). The department's decision to publish its own periodical (the *Interstate Bulletin*) also placed the department in professional struggle with the AAAE's *Journal of Adult Education* for respect, quality contributions, and readership.

Both Robert A. Luke and Knowles detail the often-contentious relationship between the department and the AAAE between 1930 and 1951, when the two organizations were merged. However, neither author addresses why the Department of Adult Education felt the need to redefine its work in 1927. After all, the existence of the AAAE would appear to lessen the need for the department to broaden its work and membership. But the

AAAE's "professional" membership served to highlight the perception that the NEA's members, affiliated as they were with a public school teaching force that remained less than "ideally" qualified, were *not* professionals. By associating the department's core membership with the already professionalized workers of libraries, art galleries, or universities, the department could hope to increase the standing of public school workers. This push for professionalization was not without its price: professionalism required the end of volunteer teaching and, along with it, the Moonlight Schools.

Deming versus Stewart, Round 2

In 1927, Robert Deming remained president of the Department of Adult Education. As detailed in chapter 4, when the Department of Immigrant Education merged with the Illiteracy Commission, Deming sent Cora Wilson Stewart a series of letters asking for her help with the new department's work. Stewart refused to offer her assistance, instead suggesting that the department's work was far broader than the task she had set for herself: the elimination of illiteracy. Though Deming at the time suggested that Stewart misunderstood the department's work, the 1927 redefinition of the department implies that Stewart was quite right to assume that illiteracy would not be the sole or even primary concern of the department as it moved forward under Deming's leadership. Though this exchange had little effect at the time—Stewart and Deming continued to pursue their individual interests, and department members followed one or the other as they preferred—the enmity this initial encounter created is one likely reason for the harsh critiques Deming launched against Stewart in his 1927 speech to the NEA's annual meeting. Deming's speech gives insight into the rationale underlying the department's crucial redefinition of its membership and of adult education.

Deming explains in the opening remarks of the department's 1927 meeting that "if ultimately the department can include in a coordinated field of adult education all those educators who instruct adults from beginning English classes to evening high school and general evening classes in special subjects, all under public auspices, it will have obtained its fullest mission" ("Department" 296). Clearly, this mission very much resembles the stated goals of the AAAE. Unlike the AAAE, Deming suggests that the attitudes of the department's membership are the primary hurdle to overcome in fulfilling this "mission":

My address today, outlining the past, present, and future of this department must take nothing for granted. There may be many here who have not my conception at all of the duties and responsibilities of state and local officials in this field of adult education, and who may not grasp that this annual meeting will probably mark the expansion of the department to include all public school education for adults. . . . You may not believe that this type of instruction [teaching English speaking and literacy] requires trained leadership to recruit and supervise classes, that trained and adequately paid teachers are essential, that a special technic and special courses of study are required. Above all, you may not believe that after flag raisings and political oratory and "reduce illiteracy by 1930" campaigns that state and local laws and appropriations are essential if anything is to actually be done. ("Department" 295)

Deming frames his beliefs as representing the future of the department, and he suggests that his beliefs differ substantially from those educators who believe that adult education should be a volunteer enterprise. Deming's reference to reducing illiteracy by 1930 is an explicit reference to Stewart's National Illiteracy Crusade, which had advertised as its mission the elimination of illiteracy before the 1930 census. Though Deming does not mention Stewart or the Moonlight Schools by name, his statement is (and would have been recognized by his audience as) a direct attack on the schools and a statement that the department would move away from the support of the schools in favor of a more professional approach to adult education.

Deming's attack is launched on two fronts. First, Deming's insistence on "trained and adequately paid teachers" necessarily implies the elimination of volunteer teaching as a source of adult education instruction. Second, though less explicit, Deming's insistence on "a special technic and special course" indicates his belief that extended study is necessary before illiterates will be able to master English speaking or literacy. The Moonlight Schools' premise was that illiterate men and women could attain basic literacy within six weeks. Deming's pronouncements imply that this claim is at best inaccurate and at worst dangerous for the work of adult educators.

Deming is not simply suggesting that Stewart's method is ineffective—he is suggesting that her influence has a negative effect on all facets of adult education. After all, if laypeople believed that any volunteer could teach literacy, adult educators could never be recognized as having special training or skills. If school districts, state agencies, and federal officials believed that illiteracy could be remedied in six weeks with no outlay of money, they would certainly not appropriate funds for longer or more extensive adult education programs. While Stewart's assertions regarding the speed and ease with which Moonlight Schools students learned to read and write were in all likelihood vastly overstated, the students' letters demonstrate that some did, in fact, learn to read and write during the short sessions of the schools. One student testifies, for instance, that he "entered the Moonlight School here Oct. 4, 1915. At that time I was unable to read or write. . . . Now after attending these school for two months I am able to read and write" (*Moonlight Schools: . . . Illiterates* 130, in image). Moreover, Stewart's volunteer teaching corps had achieved remarkable results given the lack of resources at their disposal. Had Deming's speech focused solely on Stewart's veracity, she could have produced data to discount his claims. By instead focusing on the damage Stewart's rhetoric caused the larger movement, Deming allowed that Stewart's methods *might* work, but even if—and perhaps *especially if*—the Moonlight Schools were effective, the cost of their success was simply too high for the adult education movement to bear.

Deming's emphasis on teacher training, funding, and immigrant education are reflected in the program of the annual meeting. Of the ten remaining speeches, four address only immigrant education, two address what might be called "special technics," and two others comment on "outstanding programs" of adult education, programs that employ, the speakers note, trained teachers. None of the speeches addresses illiteracy, and none focuses on native-born students.

Stewart was not scheduled to address the 1927 meeting and had no opportunity to publicly respond to Deming's assertions or to the redirection of the department as a whole. In 1928, though, Stewart used her speech to the National Council of Education (NCE) to refute Deming's claims. Her choice of audience—the NCE rather than the department—is, in itself, an indication of Stewart's disdain for the department and an attempt to emphasize her own position as a qualified educator. The NCE comprised only the most respected members of the NEA; one had to be appointed or elected to its membership by fellow educators. Deming, it is worth noting, was not a member in 1928. Stewart's ability to even address the group signaled that her expertise was established; her membership worked to counteract the implication that as an unpaid volunteer herself, she was not qualified to determine the techniques used by adult educators. In her address, Stewart critiques Deming on four points: the role of experience in developing educational theory, pedagogical methods, the relationship between professionalism and volunteerism, and the need for public campaigns.

Stewart begins by outlining the history of adult education, positing the Moonlight Schools as the "first answer" to the problem of adult illiteracy in the history of the United States. In particular, she points out that the schools had "demonstrated a fact which Dr. Thorndyke [sic] of Teachers College, Columbia University, proclaimed sixteen years later—that in the acquirement of knowledge, the grown person could outdistance the child" ("Report of the Illiteracy Committee" 247–48). Thorndike was a key figure in the adult education movement; Deming, in fact, cited Thorndike's findings to defend his own perception of the "duty for adult education" ("Department," 296). Here, Stewart suggests that her own work should be recognized as at least as revolutionary as Thorndike's and implies that her longer expertise should grant her more authority than Thorndike to testify to adults' abilities.

But Stewart's objection to professional theorists like Thorndike goes beyond personal affront. The unique benefit of the Moonlight Schools, she argues, is that they can function as a "great laboratory in which we can learn the most tactful methods and out of which we can draw suitable materials for the instruction of adult beginners" ("Report of the Illiteracy Committee" 249). Direct experience offered an effective—perhaps the only—way to determine the needs and abilities of illiterate adults, a method superior to those suggested by college professors who, Stewart implied, had theories but no actual work in the field. While training and theory could help improve methods, experience should be seen as more valuable and, in fact, essential to creating appropriate pedagogy, Stewart suggested. More important, the work of theorists and the processes of training take time; as Stewart points out, Thorndike's study was produced sixteen years after her own work had begun. In the interim, the Moonlight Schools taught thousands of illiterate adults. Stewart writes, "We shall teach many as we go on learning how best to do this rescue work. Thus would we pave the way for a better system with trained and compensated teachers" ("Report of the Illiteracy Committee" 249). The Moonlight Schools, she argues, should be viewed not as separate from theory but as a source of data from which educational theory could be built.

Adult educators did not agree. Stewart frankly outlines the divide between her supporters and Deming's:

> Two distinct methods . . . have developed in this new field of education. One group, "despising the day of small things," says, "Away with these crude pioneer methods with their spectacular and vociferous campaigning. We want no volunteer teachers. System and money are the things. We will have no schools for illiterates save those with paid teachers especially trained for teaching adults." They claim for their method stability and thoroughness. They would turn out fewer products through a longer period of school attendance, who would, according to their theory, be better trained. This group of educators would be professional rather than pioneers. ("Report of the Illiteracy Committee" 246)

Though Stewart's representation of Deming's speech is harsh, her paraphrases do reflect the core of Deming's assertions. Deming rejects volunteerism, asserting that trained, professional teachers are "essential" to the work of adult education, and he proposes longer courses targeted at smaller student populations.

Even if an equal number of students are taught, Stewart points out that Deming's model guarantees that these students will not be the men and women most in need of help:

> The results of this school or method is that it attracts a majority of educated adults and a minority of illiterates. The sessions being longer and no early goal in sight the attendance dwindles as a rule, but those who stay to the end are supposed to be well-grounded in the prescribed, but not particularly inspiring, course of study. The effect of this method on the leaders is to make them lose sight of the main objective. Illiterates become to them of diminishing importance and pupils of any degree of elementary education count as much with them as do those who have no knowledge whatsoever. ("Report of the Illiteracy Committee" 248)

Stewart's critique of the dwindling attendance of city evening schools is almost certainly drawn from Miller's and Thompson's studies of evening school conditions, though Stewart does not reference either study in her speech. Both studies found similar results—even "the most favorable figures indicate a retention of membership in evening schools not usually over one-half; the average is less—about one-third" (68). Though Thompson concludes from a survey of students who dropped out of evening schools that "there is little statistical evidence to show that the school has failed to meet the needs and expectations of the students" (97), his data set contradicts this claim. Of the eleven categories of response to the survey, only four produced more results than "discouragement about school"; two of these four were "all other reasons," a catch-all category, and "pupils not found" to be surveyed.[9] The survey also does not consider the possibility that students were reticent to critique the schools when responding to school-affiliated surveyors. In short, Stewart is in keeping with the evidence available when she suggests that adult students were "discouraged" by the coursework Americanizers proposed.

The pedagogy Stewart attributes to Americanizers is indeed discouraging. As she explains, the Americanizers' and Moonlight Schoolers' pedagogies differed in their approach to "teaching writing to beginners." The Americanizers "would first ground the adult illiterate well in penmanship, by teaching principles and movements before introducing sentences and words" ("Report of the Illiteracy Committee" 249). If this characterization accurately depicted the activities of immigrant education classes, it would be remarkable that *any* students opted to complete the courses. As explained in chapter 3, it is not possible to document the widely varied pedagogies used in Americanization classrooms; because there was no centralized authority guiding the movement, many teachers were required to create their own pedagogies in the absence of any guidance, and these pedagogies were not consistent from course to course even within one school district (Miller). Though some teachers working alone may have engaged in teaching penmanship before words (and because of the relative ease of teaching penmanship in comparison to sentence structure and vocabulary, it is likely that some teachers did), no well-known Americanization advocates supported a pedagogy of penmanship. No reference is made to such pedagogy in the NEA proceedings or among major Americanization publications. However, as Thompson's extensive study indicates, phonics were a key feature of many Americanization courses, and many students were required to learn phonics before moving on to words and sentences. As one superintendent explains, "Pupils are drilled until they understand thoroughly the phonetics and then applied on selected words for pronunciation" (Thompson 179). Thompson does not enumerate the results of his survey concerning phonics, but all of his sample "typical answers" acknowledge the use of phonics in Americanization courses. Phonics lessons are, in terms of modern pedagogical theory, far less egregious than lessons in penmanship. Yet, this emphasis on phonics functions in much the same way as Stewart's critique of penmanship. The Moonlight Schools' pedagogies held that "immediate achievement is necessary to inspire the adult beginner with selfconfidence [sic]" (Stewart, "Report of the Illiteracy Committee" 246)—an inspiration that "long-drawn-out" phonics lessons could not provide (Thompson 181).

Despite her disdain for Deming's pedagogical tenets, Stewart does not object to the idea of professionalization. She emphasizes that proponents of her method "welcome trained teachers and are glad to see them paid," and they "agree that it is good to be thorough and well to systematize" ("Report of the Illiteracy Committee" 248–49). Stewart's ideal teachers, after all, were trained day school teachers who then underwent additional training to work with adults. She also acknowledges, "We do not contend that ours is the best method" (249). But Stewart believed that Deming and his associates were putting the needs of teachers ahead of the needs of students. Volunteerism and professionalism could—and must—exist side by side. She relates, "We claim that it is the right of others to help a brother out of the ditch if they can reach him first [before trained teachers]. We regard the illiteracy movement as the Red Cross work of education, as first aid and rescue work, and urge immediate succor rather than leisurely training" (249). As explained above, the schools utilized this two-tiered model of instruction in the Rowan County literacy campaign: newly literate former students sought out illiterates to provide basic instruction and to whet their desire for education; trained teachers then worked with these illiterate students to give more in-depth instruction. Stewart also points out that some states had opted for a combination of Americanization and Moonlight Schools' methods:

> Alabama, a state which has devotedly sought the best method [for teaching illiterates] for fifteen years, swung away from an illiteracy commission a few years ago to a more standardized type of work, but recently found it advisable to create a new and volunteer state illiteracy commission. . . . This indicates that Alabama believes system and money *alone* cannot do the job. ("Report of the Illiteracy Committee" 250; emphasis added)

Combining the two models of adult education would be most beneficial to the men and women in need of instruction.

At the end of her speech, Stewart responds to Deming's primary claim—that the rhetoric of the Moonlight Schools damaged the adult education movement as a whole. She argues that because adult literacy education has not historically been a field of education, it is necessary to "dramatize itself to the public to draw adherents" ("Report of the Illiteracy Committee" 250). The effort to eradicate illiteracy is not simply a movement—it is a "war," and just as "slogans, campaign songs, posters, parades" are used to drum up support for the nation's wars, these methods should be used to provide "munitions" in the war against illiteracy (250). Stewart responds directly to Deming's critique of her campaign slogan "No Illiteracy in 1930." While this statement "may be subject to . . . criticism and jeer," as in Deming's speech, Stewart explains that "those who voice this slogan may retort to their critics 'Not failure but low aim is crime,' and may have the satisfaction of knowing that even though they may be 'the lunatic fringe' of the movement, their fanaticism has helped to bring the conservatives half way" (251). Though Deming and other adult educators might dispute the Moonlight Schools' methods, all believed that illiteracy could be eliminated through teaching adults—an inconceivable position only twenty years earlier. The fervor of Moonlight Schools advocates, Stewart suggests, is a necessary counterpoint to the rhetoric of system and training—while training may produce efficient results, campaign rhetoric is necessary to produce a *desire for* efficient results among the general public.

Stewart's response to Deming appears to have had some effect on the direction of the department. In one of his speeches to the annual meeting in the following year (1929), Deming not only specifically addresses native illiteracy but he also employs Stewart's martial rhetoric, for instance, "Thus through the census also the government is seeking ammunition for attack upon the enemy within our gates" ("Federal" 285). In his second speech, he excoriates "certain unapproved practices" used by immigrant educators, asking "Could anything be more uninspiring?" ("How" 313), echoing Stewart's critique of "discouraging" pedagogies that did not take into account adults' motivation for seeking education. Though Deming does not retreat from his stance on professionalization and systematization—one of his speeches is titled "Federal Aspects of and Responsibilities in the Reduction of Illiteracy and Training for Citizenship"—he also appears to grant

Stewart's suggestion that an essential part of adult education must be the inspiration of students and of teachers. Similarly, of the nineteen speeches department members gave to the department's annual meeting, three focus on the importance of publicity, three address the importance of engaging curricula, and eight address adult education in rural communities.

The marked shift in the department's rhetorical focus between 1928 and 1929 suggests that had Deming continued to guide policy, the department might have come to support the position Stewart recommended: a two-pronged educational method utilizing both volunteers and trained professionals. But at the 1929 meeting, Deming was replaced as department president by the Office of Education's specialist in adult education, Lewis R. Alderman. Alderman was both more concerned with illiteracy than Deming—his speeches to the NEA's annual meetings frequently reference illiteracy—and was more committed to the idea that "adult education is more than [literacy education]. This is merely foundation work. Adult education, in reality, means the development of life to the full" ("Adult" 133). As such, he believed that *all* adults should attend at least one evening class a week. He also agreed wholeheartedly with Deming's emphasis on professionalization, systematization, and research. At the first annual meeting under Alderman's leadership, the only speeches given were on the topics of research and leisure education. Alderman also set the standard of "literacy" far higher than Stewart believed appropriate. At the 1929 meeting, Alderman approved a statement of "position and policy" (coauthored by Deming) suggesting that the aim of illiteracy programs should be "fourth grade literacy" and arguing that these programs "should not be entered into with the idea of its completion in a short time, but should be sustained through a period of years, with adequately trained teachers and under State supervision" (Smith, Burnett, Grace, Deming, and Castle). Later, as the director of the New Deal Federal Emergency Relief Agency, Alderman "classified as illiterate anyone with less than a sixth-grade education" (Nelms 182). This standard, Stewart suggested, discouraged many adults from even attempting to become literate and devalued the hard-earned literacy of many others. Under Alderman's direction, the department moved further toward a professional, research-based model of practice and came increasingly in conflict with the AAAE. But (to employ Stewart's martial metaphor) the department was not the last battleground in the war between volunteerism and professionalism in literacy education: the rise and fall of the National

Advisory Commission on Illiteracy (NACI) was the final defeat for the Moonlight Schools and the volunteer-based education they advocated.

The NACI: Volunteerism versus Technique

Stewart and her fellow Moonlight Schools advocates believed that "the U.S. government [should] take the lead" in teaching illiterates, acting as "an example to the rest of the world" (Baldwin 175). In 1929, Stewart began talks with President Herbert Hoover to create a government-sponsored organization to eliminate illiteracy. In response, the Department of the Interior created the National Advisory Commission on Illiteracy (NACI). Stewart hoped that the NACI would "put power into the movement at this time and help us in a big, final battle before the census in May 1930" (Stewart, Letter to Herbert Houston, 28 Oct. 1929). Instead, the NACI became the site of the big, final battle between Moonlight Schools supporters and professionalization advocates.

The NACI's membership was appointed by Secretary of the Interior Ray Wilbur. As Stewart describes, Wilbur was "a higher institution man, which naturally [put] him in sympathy with the people of that type and their ideas" (Stewart, Letter to Henry Allen, 3 Dec. 1930). Because Wilbur himself supported the movement toward professionalization, the NACI's membership included equal numbers of "professionals in the field of adult education" (Baldwin 176) and volunteerism advocates. Stewart feared that Wilbur "may lean toward the view of [technique committee chairman] Dr. [C. R.] Mann, who favors *studying* illiteracy. It is well to study, but such an announced purpose would start the Commission off as a research body, which would not appeal to the imagination of the country at all" (Stewart, Letter to Henry Allen, 17 Oct. 1929).

Wilbur's vision of the commission's work bears out Stewart's fears. Rather than a single-minded push to end illiteracy, Wilbur charged the commission with seven tasks:

> First, that the Committee is to act so that it can render advice to the National Advisory Committee on Education; second, to agree upon a plan of procedure to ascertain necessary facts; third, to find out what has been done in the United States to combat illiteracy; fourth, to formulate an acceptable technique of training adults to overcome the handicap of illiteracy; fifth, to agree upon a method of

handling important classes of illiterates, namely, the Negro group, the immigrant group, the Indian group, and the white group; sixth, to decide upon the relationship of Americanization and illiteracy; and seventh, to take account of all important factors bearing upon the question of illiteracy. ("National Advisory Committee" 322)

In addition, Wilbur appointed a "committee on technique" to "study and proffer the best method of training the illiterate how to read and write" (322). The "technique people," as Stewart began to call professionalization-oriented adult educators, appeared poised to take control of the commission's work. Stewart and her allies on the commission—particularly, Cosmos Broadcasting Company president Herbert Houston, former North Dakota governor R. A. Nestos, and Louisiana state school superintendent T. H. Harris—combined their efforts in an attempt to keep the commission's focus on the immediate problem of teaching illiterates.

Conflicts between the two factions of the NACI arose immediately. In January 1930, less than a month after the commission's first meeting, Wilbur suggested that the commission add Elizabeth Woodward as a member. Nearly as well-known as Stewart, Woodward was famous for her work on Americanization for the NEA and was a driving force behind the creation of the Department of Immigrant Education. Stewart believed Woodward's nomination represented "another effort of a certain group [the technique people] to get control" (Stewart, Letter to R. A. Nestos, 9 Jan. 1930). Whether the move was calculated or not, Woodward certainly supported the adult educators on the committee, as many of their positions derived from her early work in surveying Americanization methods (Luke 53–54). Despite Stewart's objections, Woodward was added to the committee, though she does not seem to have wielded the level of influence Stewart expected (perhaps because Stewart, wielding one of her favorite strategies, scheduled meetings when Woodward could not attend). The NACI was also hampered by another firm professionalization advocate: Alderman. As Stewart explains, "Of the group of states where [Alderman] is most influential and has identified himself most closely with Directors of Adult Education and Americanization only one state—Pennsylvania—is cooperating. South Carolina, which he has urged as the place where we should look for leadership in fighting illiteracy, made no move to cooperate" until Stewart appealed to an influential family (Stewart, Letter to Dr. Finley).

Though her success in pushing South Carolina to cooperate indicates that Stewart still carried a great deal of influence, within the NACI her authority had already begun to wane. Rather than confront Stewart on issues of method, the adult educators, including Secretary Wilbur, simply refused to discuss these issues with Stewart at all, positioning her as a "campaigner" rather than as an "educator" who might usefully contribute to discussions of pedagogy or research. As Stewart incredulously explains to Houston, Wilbur instructed her to give the director of the NACI, M. S. Robertson, "some guidance on the general aspects of the work, but not on the educational" (Stewart, Letter to Herbert Houston, 23 May 1930). Stewart points out that "it would seem a little strange if one who has guided other nations on their illiteracy problems in four world conferences would not be expected to guide a new Director of our Committee on educational matters" (Stewart, Letter to R. A. Houston). Later, Wilbur revealed to Stewart that members of the technique committee "consider[ed her] a 'propagandist and crusader' instead of an educator" (Stewart, Letter to Henry Allen, 3 Dec. 1930). It was Stewart's very fame as an illiteracy advocate that required the advocates of professionalization to devalue her authority as an educator; so long as she was recognized as an expert, her volunteer method would remain the public face of adult education.

In her analysis of the professionalization of English studies, Anne Ruggles Gere suggests that in order to professionalize,

> would-be academics had to discredit clubwomen's literary projects in favor of their own; they stigmatized the literacy practices of women's clubs to enhance those of professors. . . . Ridicule, coupled with policies of exclusion, usually enabled male professionals to discredit and diminish female competition. (214)

Similarly, in order to cement their own status as professional academics, the adult educators on the NACI stigmatized the (mostly female) volunteer teaching corps of the Moonlight Schools, ridiculed Stewart's campaign methods, and excluded her from discussions of pedagogy. Framing Stewart as a "crusader" allowed the technique committee to avoid her influence and increased their own prestige as professionals.

Throughout 1930, the NACI moved toward a professional, antivolunteer model of instruction. In February, the group's secretary, Rufus Weaver, called for a "permanent program of eradication of adult illiteracy under the exclusive direction of the educational forces of each state" (Nestos, Letter to Stewart, 22 Feb. 1930). Two elements of this proposition appalled Stewart and her followers: "permanent" and "exclusive." Stewart believed that one key difference between her own work and that of the Americanizers was that eradicating illiteracy was a specific goal that could be achieved in a set amount of time; while she supported permanent adult education opportunities, she felt this was not the work the NACI was created to encourage. Also, if adult education was the exclusive province of the state, all efforts would have to be organized through the bureaucracy of state government. As Stewart knew from her experience working with the Kentucky legislature, innumerable hurdles would delay the teaching of illiterates if states held exclusive control. Nestos advised Stewart, "For the next couple of years at least, and as much longer as it will take the various states to enact the required laws and to improve the mental attitude of the educational forces in combatting the problem of adult illiteracy, we must continue our volunteer organization" (Nestos, Letter to Stewart, 22 Feb. 1930).

Though Weaver ultimately lost much of his power within the NACI due to a clash with Secretary Wilbur over the limits of his authority, his views reflected those of the technique committee and heralded the results of their work. These results were presented to the commission in May 1930 in the form of a manual for teaching illiterate adults. In its initial draft, the manual "outlined a course covering 192 hours" of instruction—hardly the "short cut for teaching illiterates" that the techniques committee had been charged with producing (Stewart, Letter to T. H. Harris). Perhaps more important, the first twenty-four lessons of the manual were not adequate for teaching total illiterates; Stewart relates, "It includes the writing of three letters and is supposed to leave them able to write their own letters and to read fairly well" (Stewart, Letter to R. A. Nestos, 11 Sept. 1930).[10] Stewart believed that such a lengthy course, backloaded as it is with advanced educational topics, placed the NACI "into the field of adult education" and that such a course would be entirely impractical for the unpaid, volunteer teachers she still imagined as the shock troops in her war against illiteracy (Stewart, Letter to T. H. Harris).

Stewart seems to have recognized that the manual represented a "last stand" for volunteer teaching. Her name was the one most associated with the NACI; should the commission print the manual as originally proposed, she would be seen as endorsing a professionalized model of adult education. More crucial, Stewart could not hope to effectively oppose a government-mandated plan for educating illiterates; even if individual educators continued to endorse the Moonlight Schools method, locating adequate funding would be nearly impossible—the money would go to those educators using the approved, professionalized methodology.

In light of these concerns, Stewart began lobbying all members of the NACI to reject the manual as written. She and Nestos believed:

> If the Committee on Techniques will give us a twenty-four lesson, forty-eight hour course, or a thirty-six, seventy-two as a standard, which intelligently and enthusiastically taught will enable an adult to write his name, write simple domestic letters and read fourth grade English or the social column at least in the local paper, and leave any further course merely as a continuation to be urged upon those that have completed the course that eliminates illiteracy, I am sure that the task will not be thought so formidable but that tens of thousands of teachers and hundreds of thousands of pupils will make a determined effort. (Nestos, Letter to Stewart, 15 Sept. 1930)

Stewart offered a revision of the manual that condensed the first eight chapters into four. This change effectively halved the recommended number of hours for basic literacy instruction, making the course nearly the same length as a Moonlight Schools session (Stewart, Letter to R. A. Nestos, 31 May 1930).

The techniques committee rejected Stewart's suggestions almost entirely. The only concession made to the original draft was a note informing teachers that the lessons in the text could be broken up into several different courses, allowing the basic course material to, in theory, be used as a stand-alone text. But while the committee acknowledges that teachers would "find the directions for the first period helpful in conducting a course of twenty-four lessons," as Stewart had insisted, the committee also asserts, "The Sub-Committee on Techniques is convinced that the whole series of lessons is desirable. . . . [N]o community should . . . consider its obligation in this matter completely met until all of its citizens have attained the degree of achievement defined by the entire series outlined in the manual" (W. S. Gray 6–7). The manual explicitly endorses professionalism among adult educators, insisting that the "characteristics" considered in selecting teachers should include "general professional training such as is provided in two- and four-year curriculums for teachers" and "specific training relating definitely to the problems of teaching" (23). Though the content of the lessons provided derives much from Stewart's work (and, in fact, some lessons are taken directly from Stewart's readers), her textbooks are not among those recommended at the end of each section of the manual. Moreover, the initial course alone represents at least forty-eight hours of lessons—the length Stewart had recommended for the entire manual.

Ultimately Stewart and her allies were betrayed by NACI chairman M. S. Robertson, who gave the techniques committee the vote they needed to publish the manual over Stewart's objections. Robertson had helped Stewart compose her revision, and he had been appointed chairman at Stewart's urging, because she believed him to be a staunch supporter of the Moonlight Schools. However, Robertson felt that Stewart defined the NACI's work too narrowly—his task, he believed, was to oversee all aspects of adult education, not just the education of absolute illiterates. In light of Robertson's "desertion," Stewart felt that "the only thing . . . to do was to let the manual go to the printer" (Stewart, Letter to R. A. Nestos, 11 Sept. 1930). If she refused, she would, in effect, have publicly acknowledged her lack of power within the commission and, more pressingly, she might have given potential donors "the impression of dissention at the NACI" (Baldwin 179). Given the lack of adequate governmental funds, the NACI could not even hope to print the disputed manual without private money; no one on the commission could afford to alienate donors, but Stewart's position was particularly precarious because she had no institutional or governmental affiliation to rely on if the commission became impotent.

Shortly after the manual's publication, Stewart took extreme measures to regain control of the NACI. She convinced her supporter Harris to create a job for Robertson and agreed to secretly pay Robertson's salary from her own pocket. Robertson removed, Stewart carefully scheduled an executive committee meeting to elect a new director at a time when all of her supporters could attend and some adult education proponents could not, guaranteeing her ascension to the directorship. However, this was "a Pyrrhic victory" (Nelms 173). Though Stewart held control, she could procure no funds with which to enact any programs or campaigns; she had difficulty even paying traveling expenses for members of the executive committee to attend NACI meetings. Perhaps most telling, Stewart convinced the Rosenwald Fund to provide a $5,000 grant, but in order to receive the money, Stewart had to produce $5,000 in matching funds within one year—a mark the NACI could not come close to achieving, in spite of an extension the fund granted. Completely impotent, the NACI was discontinued after Franklin D. Roosevelt's election.

Students for Teachers, Not Teachers for Students

Adult educators were not unique in their drive for professionalization. Throughout the United States, nearly all pursuits became increasingly professionalized in the late nineteenth and early twentieth centuries. Eliot Freidson explains that during the period, "A large number of tasks which were originally performed on a voluntary basis by amateurs or performed for personal or household use rather than for a market are now performed by full-time workers who gain their living thereby" (109). Magali Sarfatti Larson suggests that this shift toward professionalism resulted from the rise of a corporate model of capitalism. She indicates that "large productive units [like corporations], characterized by high ratios of fixed capital per worker and high productivity, need to plan and regulate production, distribution and employment to ensure profits," which spawned "administrative structures [that] emphasize[d] expert decision-making" (137). Perhaps more important, the rise of corporations led to "the decline of small entrepreneurs and independent workers" (137). Rather than broad, experientially based expertise, narrow, credential-based expertise became the currency of the job market. Between 1880 and 1930, almost all (of what we now consider) professions underwent a process of increasing specialization, including law (see Powell), social work (see Lowe and Reid), nursing (see Whelan), and economics (see Maloney) and within the university, mathematics (see Dauben and Scriba) and history (see Kramer, Reid, and Barney), among others. Adult education was but one battleground in a far-larger conflict between an ethos of volunteerism and the drive toward increasing specialization. Given the overwhelming societal push toward professionalization, it is not surprising that Stewart and the Moonlight Schools lost support to professional adult educators.

Like other professions, educators pushed toward professionalization in the first three decades of the twentieth century. But the "rural school problem" presented a seemingly insurmountable obstacle. It was simply not possible to insist on trained, specialist teachers when Kentucky alone required eight thousand elementary teachers. To lessen the number of rural school teachers, state governments (under pressure from the NEA) passed legislation encouraging or requiring the consolidation of school districts. In Illinois, for instance, "4,000 of the 10,071 schools had 15 or less pupils" (Ellsworth 119); if these schools could be joined even to create thirty-pupil classrooms, the state would require two thousand fewer teachers. Consolidation moved slowly, especially in Kentucky, due to local resistance—many rural communities resisted the removal of schools (and residents' tax dollars) to other districts—and, more important, poor roads. But the push to consolidate schools often drove infrastructure improvements; as Kentucky's rural school supervisor explained in 1917, "Good roads improve transportation: improved transportation makes possible [the] consolidation of district schools; consolidation invariably improves the schools" (qtd. in Angelo). By 1950, Kentucky had only 3,462 one-room schoolhouses, which represented a substantial reduction from 1910 (Ellsworth 128). Increasing state and federal involvement in education also led to higher standards for teachers. The competition created by the reduction of teaching posts and the more rigorous certification processes led to an increasingly professionalized corps of teachers, and improved infrastructure allowed more rural teachers to train at public (and private) normal schools. The push toward consolidation almost certainly cost some potential students an opportunity to attend school. Because the distances students now needed to cover to get to and from school were much greater, some students would simply have been too far from the local school building to attend regularly, particularly in winter;[11] moreover, attending a distant school would have cut further into the time children were available to work at home. However, consolidation did have positive effects on the quality of education that students received and, perhaps as important, on local infrastructure, as both state and federal governments were more willing to allocate money for roads in rural areas.

Federal involvement in education increased substantially during the Roosevelt administration. In particular, Roosevelt moved to make adult education a federally sponsored activity. His Federal Emergency Relief Administration (FERA) engaged Alderman to "direct the work" of teaching adult illiterates (Nelms 183). Alderman's selection was a clear statement that the administration saw adult education as the purview of professionals rather than volunteers, given his long-standing and vocal commitment to professionalization. But FERA was also instrumental in publicly cementing the idea that adult literacy education should be the work of professionals. As biographer Willie Nelms explains, the purpose of FERA's illiteracy education program was not to teach illiterates—though this teaching was certainly viewed as a positive boon—but rather to employ the "40,000 teachers" who were "on relief" (183). In keeping with this purpose, Alderman "announced that anyone with less than a sixth grade education could enroll in FERA literacy classes" (Nelms 183). By setting the bar so high, Alderman helped guarantee that there would be enough students to occupy a substantial number of unemployed teachers.

Stewart objected vigorously to Alderman's standard, asserting that "it would make many of our fathers and mothers illiterate" if literacy was based solely on the grade level a person had completed ("Radio Address"). What Stewart failed—or refused—to understand was that this was the point of Alderman's standard; if our fathers and mothers were illiterate, many more teachers could be employed, and many more adults could be lured back into schools. Nelms aptly describes the reversal of fortunes for teachers of adults:

> In essence, the New Deal work with illiterate adults was an upside down version of Stewart's Kentucky campaign. In the second decade of the twentieth century, she persuaded teachers to teach voluntarily in Moonlight Schools so that illiterates might learn basic skills to improve their lives. By contrast, in the 1930s, the illiterates went to school so that the economic condition of teachers could be improved. (184)

After campaigning over twenty years for federal support for adult literacy education, Stewart's movement was ultimately doomed by its achievement. Because the government was perceived as providing all necessary services, Stewart could find no funding and few volunteers for her campaigns, and her National Illiteracy Crusade was defunct by the end of 1934. The FERA literacy education programs finalized a public perception of adult literacy education as the work of trained professionals subsidized by state or national authorities. Volunteers were not encouraged and would not have been welcome—their presence would have meant fewer students for government-employed teachers.

Most important, Alderman's inflation of the literacy standard marked the effective death of the idea that "anyone can teach." By marking anyone with less than a sixth-grade education as not only uneducated but actually illiterate, Alderman and, by extension, the government denied the worth of basic education. The further one proceeded in organized schooling, the more one's education—and, by extension, oneself—counted, but the counter did not begin until one had achieved basic education. Expertise was no longer marked by ability, as in the traditional census reference to a literate person as one "able to read" or "able to write," but by educational attainment. Respect and status migrated from the demonstration of skills to the demonstration of credentials. Being able to read and write no longer suggested any ability or any *right* to instruct an illiterate person.

Adult educators achieved professionalization through a process of exclusion that closely mirrors the professionalization of English studies that Gere describes. By redefining the meaning of "literacy," adult educators created a dichotomy between themselves and the general public, effectively creating a student body—a student body that then served to justify the existence of specialized adult educators. By marginalizing, ignoring, and denigrating the work of volunteers, adult educators created a public image of adult education as a lengthy, difficult process that required the expertise of specialized educators. Much like the clubwomen who were made "fearful they were reading the wrong books or reading them in the wrong ways" (Gere 217), untrained volunteers were left with the impression that they might do more harm than good if they attempted to teach illiterates. Highly trained, professional instructors came to be recognized as the best and often only possible source of literacy education, even within volunteer organizations—organizations that now provide extensive training for potential instructors before placing them in the classroom.

6. IMPLICATIONS AND CONCLUSIONS

𝓔he Moonlight Schools and Americanizers responded to a public discourse of literacy crisis that framed illiteracy as a threat to American identity. In particular, both immigrants and Appalachians were imagined as unable to participate in "literate society" and thus unsuitable for democratic citizenship. Less explicitly, both immigrants and Appalachians were imagined as threats to a public narrative that attributed economic and social success to individual effort and achievement: the existence of a large underclass who, as a group, lacked the tools necessary to rise to middle-class status threatened this meritocratic narrative.

The Moonlight Schools and Americanizers responded to these discourses of literacy crisis by creating pedagogies and counter-rhetorics that posited adult students as educable. In doing so, the two movements spawned a public rhetoric of literacy education that framed—and continues to frame—the disciplinary identity of literacy educators. The previous chapters illustrate the approaches taken by the Moonlight Schools and Americanizers and the public rhetoric that both shaped and responded to those approaches; the current chapter now explores how the history of these groups can help inform the work of literacy educators today.

The following analysis of the Moonlight Schools and Americanization offers important lessons for modern literacy educators and begins with highlighting the role the Moonlight Schools and Americanizers played in the development of literacy studies as a scholarly discipline. Despite this essential role, perhaps the greatest significance of the Moonlight Schools and Americanization narratives lies primarily in that by reading these two narratives in parallel with other histories of literacy education, we can better understand our own attitudes toward literacy and literacy instruction and develop a new lens through which to view our disciplinary work.

Direct Influences on Public Discourse

The discourse surrounding the Moonlight Schools and Americanization programs between 1910 and 1930 has had a direct influence on the public discourse within which literacy education continues to operate, and coming to understand this influence can help all literacy educators analyze how attitudes surrounding literacy education have developed and, by extension, how to alter those attitudes. Specifically, the discourse between the two groups has had a profound effect on the professionalization of literacy studies.

As illustrated in chapter 5, the rivalry between Americanization advocates and Moonlight Schools supporters centered on teacher professionalization and their perceptions of the difficulty of learning to read and write. The Americanizers argued that in order to teach adults even the basics of reading and writing, teachers should be trained, preferably through a college curriculum, in techniques designed especially for adult learners. Furthermore, Americanizers held that learning to read and write was a long-term commitment—typically several years—and should begin with the most basic elements of written texts (letters), regardless of student interest or engagement. The Moonlight Schools, conversely, insisted that any literate person could teach reading and writing (though training would make this teaching more thorough and efficient) and that reading and writing could be learned in as few as three weeks.

The debate between the Moonlight Schools adherents and Americanizers generated much discussion in popular discourse, particularly among educators: the NEA's *Addresses and Proceedings* regularly featured discussions that both explicitly and tacitly explored professionalization of teaching writing and of adult education. In the last years of the 1920s, these debates entered governmental rhetoric, as congressmen, official appointees, and Presidents Hoover and Roosevelt sought to frame the work first of the National Advisory Committee on Illiteracy (NACI) and later of the Federal Emergency Relief Administration (FERA). Ultimately, the Americanizers' view of adult education became instantiated as government policy: FERA defined "literate" as the equivalent of a sixth-grade education and offered teachers monetary incentives to enroll in training programs. This policy not only worked to destroy the momentum of the Moonlight

Schools movement—because government funding was available for teachers, few could be induced to answer the Moonlight Schools' call for volunteer teaching—but also ensured that adult literacy education would be perceived as a long-term enterprise carried out by specially trained instructors.

The battle between the Moonlight Schools and Americanizers, as well as its results, carries two specific and direct consequences for literacy instructors today. First, the public debate sparked by the two movements permanently altered perceptions of the qualifications necessary to teach reading and writing, yet paradoxically also perpetuated the belief that teaching reading and writing was not difficult. Second, the shift from a widely accepted definition of "literacy" as the basic skills of reading and writing to a more limited definition that set the bar much higher set the terms for later discussions of literacy and for rhetorics of literacy crises. Below, I examine these consequences and their continued impact on the work of literacy educators.

The Development of Professional Literacy Teaching

To attribute a sea change in literacy instruction to two independent, largely extra-institutional literacy programs may appear a radical suggestion from a present-day perspective, at a time when researchers in nearly every institution of higher learning are engaged in the study of reading and writing and at least three disciplines—education, literature, and composition studies—consider literacy research a key part of their disciplinary purview. However, conditions in 1910, the year before the first Moonlight Schools course and several years after the first well-documented Americanization courses were begun, were quite different. Nila Banton Smith reminds us that between 1885 and 1910, only thirty-four scientific studies of reading had been conducted in the United States (147). After 1909, when Thorndike published a handwriting scale that marks "the beginning of the contemporary movement for scientifically measuring educational products," a plethora of scientific investigations into reading and, far less often, writing was undertaken (147). The lack of scientific studies reflects a lack of theorization of literacy instruction, in general; while many theorists developed pedagogical methods to *improve* students' reading and writing, almost no theoretical work examined how to *initially* teach students to interpret or construct meaningful signs on paper. The man heralded among education scholars as the "father of reading research," William S.

Gray, did not publish anything until 1915. Indeed, prior to 1910, the only requirement placed on elementary school teachers in most states was that they had completed high school and could read and write. Even if reading research had existed, the teachers charged with imparting initial literacy instruction to students would not have been familiar with it.

The lack of reading research prior to 1910 stemmed from a widespread belief, as expressed by the Massachusetts House Committee on Education in 1834, "that every person, who has himself undergone a process of instruction, must acquire, by that very process, the art of instructing others" (Dodge 183). Hence, the lone test for potential elementary educators was a literacy test. If one had learned to read, one could teach reading; if one could write, one could teach writing. Because literacy was not perceived as difficult to acquire or to teach, there seemed to be no rationale and little public desire for pursuing a better or more efficient way to teach it. In the words of James Gee's twenty-first-century theorization of literacy, "[M]ost children learn to read, regardless of what instructional approach a school adopts, as long [as] it is not particularly stupid" (7). The same was true of schooled children in the nineteenth and early twentieth centuries: they, too, seemed to learn to read without particular effort on the part of educators or educational theorists.

The immigrant literacy crisis that erupted in the first decade of the twentieth century and the concomitant "revelation" that a substantial number of "Anglo-Saxon," native-born Americans were also illiterate increased public discussion of literacy education to a fevered pitch. Educational programs did not exist to deal with the millions of adult illiterates suddenly thrust into public discourse, nor were elementary educators equipped to address second-language education for immigrant children. Indeed, Americans, particularly educators, came to realize that there was no standard against which to measure immigrant literacy; as Sharlip and Owens explain, Americanizers could not come to an agreement on what should be taught in their basic education classes, nor could they agree on what standard of literacy attainment (or any other educational attainment) would be considered sufficient for immigrants. The immigrant and Appalachian literacy crises of the early twentieth century created, in a very real sense, the concept of literacy theory and research in an effort to create these standards.

The Americanization movement and the Moonlight Schools were the first and, for some time, the only answer to the "problem" of adult illiteracy.

As such, both organizations played a major role in shaping the nascent field of literacy studies. Nearly all of the leading basic literacy researchers participated directly in one or both of the movements, including James McKeen Cattell, Gray, Edward Lee Thorndike, and Robert Sessions Woodworth (see Willis; Sears; Berger et al.). Furthermore, because the Moonlight Schools and Americanization were deliberately created in public discourse in ways that elementary education was not—that is, both Stewart and prominent Americanizers set out to ensure that their movements were (favorably) covered by the press—the two movements shaped public perceptions of what literacy entailed and how literacy should be taught. Proponents of the Moonlight Schools and Americanizers remained the dominant voices in public discussions of literacy until the late 1920s, when the problem of adult illiteracy was perceived to have been largely "solved" by the creation of literacy requirements and quota laws for immigration and of improved public schooling opportunities for minority and rural populations. As the two adult-oriented movements waned, professional, college-based researchers of education gained prominence as the leading voices of literacy theory, and the site of research on literacy shifted to childhood learning.

Although the Americanization and Moonlight Schools movements were relatively short-lived, their position at the forefront of the establishment of literacy research as a credible, useful enterprise gave the organizations a disproportionately large role in shaping public perceptions of what it meant—and means—to teach literacy skills. In particular, the two movements were highly invested in promoting specific ideas of who could teach writing. As discussed in chapter 5, the Americanization movement promoted the professionalization of adult education; literacy, the movement's proponents said, could and should only be taught by those specifically trained to teach it. The Moonlight Schools argued the opposite: literacy could and should be taught by any literate person to any illiterate person. Though special training would improve the quality of instruction, all literate people were capable of providing the rudiments of instruction.

In taking this position, Stewart and her teachers echoed the widespread beliefs, active in the century prior to the schools' formation, that any persons who had themselves been taught to read could impart that instruction to others and that literacy could be achieved with relatively little effort by any motivated learner. In *Moonlight Schools: For the Emancipation of Adult Illiterates*, for instance, Stewart quotes an "eminent psychologist": "I have always believed, that reading, writing and arithmetic are comparatively easy subjects for the adult mind" (28). The promotion of an "anyone can teach" approach to basic literacy education carried benefits and drawbacks for the Moonlight Schools and adult illiterates: certainly, this approach maximized the number (if not the quality) of educational opportunities available to illiterate men and women; however, this approach also guaranteed that funding, particularly from public sources, would be difficult to obtain. After all, if anyone could teach, why would special funds need to be allocated for literacy instruction?

Although the belief that anyone could teach literacy had been firmly entrenched throughout the history of American education, the Moonlight Schools played a crucial role in promoting this attitude. Previously, the belief that "anyone could teach" was a convenient belief based on anecdotal evidence: children learned to read despite their teachers' lack of special training; therefore, reasoning went, anyone could teach literacy. Furthermore, it was not until the widespread development of normal schools and, in the last decade of the nineteenth century, teachers' colleges that an actual alternative to the idea that anyone could teach had existed. Even after the development of teachers' colleges, few rural teachers—who made up the majority of elementary educators in the United States—could afford to enroll. The view that anyone could teach was rarely a conscious choice among multiple alternatives but more often represented acquiescence to an unavoidable state of affairs. The Moonlight Schools, then, granted legitimacy to the idea that anyone could teach, by developing rhetorical appeals that specifically promoted volunteer, untrained teachers *against* a viable alternative rhetoric of professionalization, formalizing what had previously been a "common sense" approach to education.

Conversely, the very existence of millions of illiterate adults gave credence to Americanizers' drive for professionalization. Clearly, the educational system had failed in some way; while the NEA ensured that much of the blame for adult illiteracy was placed on the poor material conditions of schools, teachers received much of the blame as well. Working with education researchers, many of whom were employed by teachers' colleges, Americanizers argued that just as education theorists like Dewey were employing special techniques in the teaching of children, so, too, was a "special technic" necessary for teaching adults (Deming, "Department" 302).

Unlike Stewart, whose rhetorical approach relied primarily on testimonial and visual evidence, Americanizers employed a rhetoric of science. To develop and implement "special technics," Americanizers developed mutually supportive relationships with literacy researchers (and, indeed, literacy researchers were often themselves tacit or explicit Americanizers),[1] and the scientific appeals of literacy researchers furnished the rhetorical support for Americanizers' arguments. Between 1910 and 1920, literacy researchers developed a variety of tests that claimed to objectively assess students' literacy skills, beginning with the aforementioned Thorndike handwriting scale. The two most famous tests were Gray's Standard Oral Reading Paragraphs (1915), the first "standardized reading test"[2] (N. B. Smith 151) and the Army Alpha and Beta intelligence tests (1917). Though the army tests were not explicitly tests of literacy, they were nevertheless used by Stewart, Americanizers, and literacy researchers alike to make broad claims about the standards and uses of literacy in the United States. Stewart's choice to rely on testimonial evidence for the success of volunteer teaching methods almost certainly contributed to the Moonlight Schools' demise: in an era of professionalization and increasing scientism in all fields, her evidentiary appeals rang increasingly hollow. That Stewart was able to maintain public interest and support for so long was partially due to a major gap in literacy research: despite the widespread use of the army intelligence tests as "evidence" of literacy skills, no substantial research had been conducted to directly test the processes of literacy acquisition in adults.[3] Given her rhetorical emphasis on the differences between child and adult learning styles, Stewart could adequately combat the Americanizers' appeals to a scientific program of education and teacher training on the grounds that her evidence spoke directly to the issue of teaching adults.

This state of affairs changed in 1928, the year before the founding of the NACI. Once again, Thorndike led the way: his 1927 *The Measurement of Intelligence* and 1928 *Adult Learning* used commonly accepted testing practices to assert that adults were capable of learning, though at a slower rate than children. Gray, likewise, had begun investigations into the nature of adult literacy and learning, though his results had not yet been published. Following Thorndike's 1927 publication of adult literacy research, Robert Deming of the NEA's Department of Adult Education launched his attack against Stewart's volunteer-based methods. Thorndike's findings, which suggested that adults could, in fact, learn more than children but needed longer periods of instruction to do so, fully substantiated Americanizers' program of instruction: since adults could learn advanced subjects, well-trained teachers were necessary, and because adults required longer learning times, extensive programs of study were needed.

The success of the Americanizers' appeals was evident in the formation of the NACI. Though the commission had been Stewart's idea, many of the commission members, much to her chagrin, were drawn from among literacy researchers and their supporters—a signal that scientific appeals were more persuasive to the federal government than her testimonial evidence. Moreover, the immediate task assigned to the NACI was to "study and proffer the best method of training the illiterate how to read and write" ("National Advisory Committee" 322); that is, the mandate was not to teach or support the teaching of literacy, as Stewart had wished, but, rather, to study the processes of literacy education scientifically.

By 1933, the Moonlight Schools and the NACI were defunct. The final death knell for Stewart's volunteer movement came with the institution of professional teacher-training programs through FERA in 1933 and concomitant availability of free basic education to adults. Once again, literacy research and professionalization efforts—now guided by "adult educators," many of whom had previously identified as Americanizers—worked hand-in-hand: in 1933, FERA's director, Lewis R. Alderman, argued that those with the equivalent of a sixth-grade education should be considered literate; in 1935, Gray's long-awaited *What Makes a Book Readable*, with its extensive study of adult reading practices, created a standardized scale of grade-level equivalencies that could then be used to substantiate and support FERA's assertions about literacy standards.

Denaturalizing "Common Sense" Narratives

In addition to these direct historical influences, the Moonlight Schools and Americanization narratives provide an opportunity for literacy educators to read these narratives against other, similar historical narratives and to remind ourselves that such histories *are* narratives. That is, previous chapters have offered a historical narrative of the Moonlight Schools and Americanization movements; however, the archival evidence available ultimately determines the narrative I can offer of the movements' histories. I recognize that the archives likely participate in eliding differences, particularly because Stewart herself had a hand in editing the contents of the Moonlight Schools archival material. Furthermore, as any historian must, I have chosen to emphasize particular elements of the Moonlight Schools' history that are relevant to my project of enriching our historical understanding of literacy education; for instance, I have chosen not to focus on Stewart's relationships with fellow reformers or her personal political inclinations because little extant evidence suggests that either factor played a determining role in the schools' rhetoric or pedagogy.

The narrative I have chosen focuses on elements of the Moonlight Schools and Americanization particularly relevant to composition studies, education, and adult education, the disciplines currently most involved in theorizing literacy pedagogies. Below are highlights of those elements of pedagogy, practice, and theory that offer those of us within these fields the opportunity to read our own historical understandings of literacy education against and in parallel within these alternative locations, a reading process that, as scholar Jacqueline Jones Royster argues, can help further illuminate each group's history and practices.

The Moonlight Schools and Americanization narratives can help move the history of literacy education toward an approach less focused on traditional schooling models and more focused on literacy in all of its settings. By shifting focus away from the university as the exclusive site of both adult literacy education and the development of student-centered literacy pedagogies, the narratives of the Moonlight Schools and Americanization can broaden the field's scope and vision to include alternative sites of literacy education and innovation.

The Moonlight Schools and Americanization narratives are valuable in challenging a historical model of literacy education that centers on traditional schooling in two ways. First, by virtue of their very existence, their aim to teach underserved student populations, and, in the case of the Moonlight Schools, its recognition of student agency and its development of adult-oriented primers, the movements represent a gold mine of pedagogical innovation at a time that historical narratives of both K–12 and college literacy education insist was a theoretical and pedagogical wasteland of "current-traditional" pedagogy that relied on theme writing and drills (see Berlin; Cremin; Crowley). Second, because the Moonlight Schools *did* employ elements of "current-traditional pedagogy"—students participated in oral drills on a number of subjects, including grammar and elocution—yet also recognized student agency within the implementation of those elements by asking students to participate with teachers in selecting drill subjects, the Moonlight Schools' narrative works to illustrate that even those aspects of current-traditional pedagogy that appear most harmful to students' agency within the classroom could, in practice, function as a site of collaboration and negotiation.

Reading the narratives of the Moonlight Schools and Americanization can thus enable more nuanced understandings of the history of literacy instruction and, in so doing, can help us articulate more positive images of our students, of the field of literacy education, in general, and of such disciplines as composition studies and education, specifically. Both narratives work to highlight the differences among adults' and children's educational needs and to remind us that our students are now, and have historically been, adults who bring legitimate and valuable desires, goals, knowledges, and literacies to our classrooms. Historical narratives that frame our students as equally knowledgeable in their interactions with us—albeit in different areas of expertise—can help us reframe our future work as exchanging knowledges rather than as remediating lack.

The Moonlight Schools' narrative can also serve to illuminate a historical blindness to the work done in extra-institutional literacy sites and to encourage more fruitful future research and practice. Bronwyn Williams points out, for instance, that composition studies' university- and discipline-centric approach to research and history arises in part from "the institutional and disciplinary forces that reward us for consolidating our identity as a field focused on college writing" (129). The Moonlight Schools can highlight—both for composition studies and other locations within the traditional schooling hierarchy—the intellectual loss that we risk when we fail to consult extra-institutional literacy sites. Because the Moonlight Schools were not affiliated with a university, the pedagogical theories and innovations that characterize the movement did not make their way into contemporary composition classrooms. However, the Moonlight Schools were, in fact, an innovative site of literacy instruction, and though college-based researchers did not acknowledge this fact at the time, *the general public did*. In an intellectual sense, we can easily imagine how the movement's theories and pedagogies could have benefited contemporary K–12 and college educators, particularly as those educators attempted to address their work to first- and second-generation immigrants whose educational and cultural backgrounds and languages were much different from more traditional, primarily English-speaking students. In a social sense, university-based researchers' failure to work with the Moonlight Schools lengthened and at times stymied universities' efforts to promote their vision of professionalization, legislation, and pedagogy because these researchers had to contend with the public credibility of Stewart and her movement. As we move forward as a discipline, the Moonlight Schools' narrative can illustrate what we might gain—and what we may be missing—by not engaging with extra-institutional sites of literacy education.

While the Moonlight Schools' narrative does offer these useful historical understandings and future directions, the narrative also can also illustrate the limits of particular practices and rhetorical frameworks. As argued in chapters 2 and 3, the rhetoric of the Moonlight Schools movement sought to explicitly credit the knowledges that students brought to the classroom and to depict illiterate people as victims of circumstance rather than innately flawed or immoral. However, the narrative of the schools—a narrative that includes not only the explicit rhetoric of its practitioners but also the tacit endorsements incorporated in their rhetoric and pedagogy—in some ways worked to further undercut the moral and ethical standing of illiterate people.

The Moonlight Schools' narrative depicts a movement with a foolproof pedagogy: if students followed the lessons Stewart and her teachers prescribed, the student would learn to read, regardless of the student's level of experience, age, or social position. Furthermore, the schools are imagined as catering to the availability of adult students: by holding classes at night, posting teachers in individuals' homes, and sending teachers into isolated communities, the schools were, in theory, available to all adults who desired education. While this rhetoric of success and opportunity certainly helped to attract students and, perhaps more important, teachers to the schools, this rhetoric also had potentially negative effects on perceptions of illiteracy. Specifically, because the schools were represented as a cure-all for illiteracy, people who remained illiterate despite the schools' presence in their communities were tacitly framed as having rejected educational opportunity and, by extension, as illiterates by choice.

The discourse of unavoidable success the Moonlight Schools employed limited their ability to recognize and account for differences among adults within the same community and to appreciate the cultural and psychological ramifications of engaging in an educational process. Although Stewart was perhaps more aware than other educators of her time of the differences in learning styles between children and adults and among different cultural communities, her textbooks and rhetoric demonstrate little awareness or discussion of learning styles: the assumption inhering in all of her textbooks is that members of the same community will encounter texts in the same way and will learn equally well from those texts. In present-day parlance, the Moonlight Schools rhetoric leaves no way to account for learning disabilities (dyslexia, for instance), learning styles (e.g., visual, audio, kinestheic), or multiple intelligences. Although Stewart's account suggests that individual teachers *did* seek to account for these differences, the larger public narrative of the schools did not recognize these efforts. Instead, because the Moonlight Schools courses were framed as infallible, any student's failure to achieve literacy through the courses was not acknowledged in public discourse and, as such, was imagined as a failure by the student rather than the program itself.

The rhetoric of the Moonlight Schools movement also ignores the cultural contest that occurs in the process of education, particularly as employed by the Moonlight Schools. Stewart herself acknowledges that her textbooks are designed to impel students to adopt particular values "by suggestion, if by nothing else" (*Moonlight Schools: . . . Illiterates* 72). Implying, for instance, that the appearance of one's home is a reflection on one's moral character, as *The Country Life Readers, First Book* suggests, denigrates students' existing practices, beliefs, and, literally, homes (and tacitly links poverty with poor moral character). Yet, there is no concomitant recognition that because students' language, beliefs, and identity were threatened by the schools' attempts to inculcate middle-class values, students might resist or reject the schools' educational project. The schools did make a concerted effort to avoid framing students as "at fault" for their illiteracy, and Stewart even goes so far as to place blame for students' refusal to attend class on the schools: she writes that some illiterates "could not be induced to learn," placing the failure on the teachers seeking to induce rather than the illiterates for "refusing" to attend (*Moonlight Schools: . . . Illiterates* 55). But despite Stewart's efforts, the narrative of the schools, because it relied so heavily on a rhetoric of guaranteed success, ultimately failed to recognize and account for the cultural coercion carried out by its pedagogies and, by extension, to recognize and account for students' resistance to those pedagogies.

In incorporating the Moonlight Schools' and Americanization narratives into our disciplinary discourse, we must be aware of their limitations. The problems with the narrative of Americanization are somewhat obvious: while the groups did succeed in providing learning opportunities for immigrants, they did so at the cost of reinforcing prejudicial assumptions about language and racial difference. The Moonlight Schools' narrative, too, if not critically employed, can perpetuate a damaging process of blaming the victim for his/her "failure" to learn. But the limits of the Moonlight Schools narrative can also offer an important cautionary example for modern literacy educators. As we work to promote our discipline to the academy and the public, we are often asked to frame our work in terms of a "solution" to the perceived "problem" of student writing. In promoting our important and vibrant work, we, too, must analyze the effects of our rhetoric, finding the fine line between giving due credit to our scholarly work and recognizing that students' "failures" to respond to our pedagogies may represent flaws in our own thinking rather than in students' willingness or ability to learn.

Long-Term Effects: Who Teaches Literacy?

As a quick glance through almost any state or national newspaper will remind us, the concept of grade-level equivalencies Gray developed and Alderman incorporated into federal policy remains the preferred rubric for public and governmental discussion of literacy (as well as other subjects). Indeed, the No Child Left Behind Act uses grade-level equivalencies as the measure by which schools' performances are assessed. The concept reflected by grade-level equivalencies—that "literacy" entails a specific set of advanced skills rather than the basic process of inscription and decoding of symbols—is fully entrenched in public and academic discourse. Perhaps more important, the necessarily associated belief that teachers must be specially trained to impart literacy instruction to their students is the common sense of our educational system. Moreover, the idea that literacy—specifically, the literacy of adults—is a worthy topic and is receptive to academic research has been well established and accepted both in academia and, to a large extent, among the general public.

Professional literacy education is made possible by this set of accepted principles. Our identity as a field is predicated upon the belief that literacy is an essential subject of research, that literacy entails more than basic decoding, and that we can in some way assess literacy skills. It is not an exaggeration to say that literacy studies exists as a discipline (or, rather, as a part of many disciplines) today in part because of the work of the Moonlight Schools and Americanizers in publicizing adult literacy as a national issue and, in doing so, providing an institutional, governmental, and public rationale for the conduct and funding of extensive literacy-research efforts. If we are to grasp how educational institutions, disciplines, and the study of literacy have "changed and failed to change," reading the narratives of the Moonlight Schools and Americanization against histories of education based in traditional educational settings can help shed light on our assumptions and attitudes.

If we are to understand the scholarly field of literacy studies in relation to public perceptions of literacy—an understanding that is essential in a period of increasing demand for accountability and demonstrable results from the federal government and the general public—it is vitally important that we as a field come to understand how the "common sense" of literacy has changed over the past century. More important, we must understand the assumptions that inhere in our own definitions of "literacy" and recognize that these definitions reflect particular "givens" of education and culture that are, in fact, relatively recent social constructions.

Although the Moonlight Schools were instrumental in shaping the Americanizers'/adult educators' rhetoric and thus, paradoxically, in the widespread acceptance of the Americanizers' program of long-term instruction provided by specially trained teachers, little of the schools' rhetoric or pedagogy is evident in current discourse surrounding literacy. But there is one notable exception—an unfortunate exception, for those of us who teach literacy: though the Americanizers' call for specially trained teachers was answered by the federal training of thousands of teachers and, later, by dedicated composition studies and education faculty within universities, the view that any literate person can teach writing has maintained currency within contemporary academic and public discourse. As Sharon Crowley suggests, we need look no further than the teaching assistants who most often teach writing at colleges and universities: though these graduate students do have "special training" in literary studies, few have specific training in teaching writing or, indeed, any pedagogical training whatsoever.[4] That is, English graduate students are assumed to be qualified to teach reading and writing to college-level students—that is, adults—because *they themselves have been taught to read and write at the college level.*

In light of this attitude, literacy studies at all levels, but particularly composition studies within the university, have long struggled to establish disciplinary credibility within academia. As Cary Moskovitz and Michael Petit lament, "If anyone can teach writing, what good is a Ph.D. in Comp?" (86). Although the field has been asked to provide the "answer" to poor student writing that few other teachers feel qualified to correct or are interested in correcting, nevertheless, compositionists have historically received less respect than more established disciplines. As Mike Rose explains in 1979, "Writing research is viewed with disdain in many English departments; tenure and advancement will not come to the scholar whose concerns are not 'literary'" (277). In 1998, Crowley echoes Rose's statement, asserting that "faculty who are not professionally associated with composition instruction . . . view composition faculty as literacy gatekeepers rather than as intellectuals and teachers" and suggesting that "[d]espite its radical and ground-breaking discoveries about pedagogy, composition studies nevertheless remains almost invisible within academic hierarchies" (243). And in 2010, Gregory Colomb cautions that we must still work against defining the work of composition studies as "service" because when outsiders understand our work as service, "we and our work are too readily disrespected, both undervalued and undercompensated" (12). He also emphasizes that our field faces challenges "related to the irregular nature of our place in the academy," in part because "[c]omposition has no optimal institutional home and therefore its institutional relationship can count on no predictable expectations and can rely on no predictable best practices" (13).

Each of these commentators and many others in the past four decades have argued that composition studies' identification with teaching the first-year writing course has prevented the field from achieving disciplinary status within the academy and from gaining respect from other academics. Both Crowley and Colomb argue that composition studies' identity as a "service discipline" rather than a research discipline has worked against recognition of composition studies as a site of knowledge creation. That is, composition studies' primary work—"teaching writing"—is not perceived as producing specialized knowledge.

While I concur with Crowley and Colomb, I argue that analyzing composition studies' disciplinary identity through the lens of the Moonlight Schools' narrative can further illuminate contemporary perceptions of teaching writing. Like composition studies, the Moonlight Schools were perceived solely as a site of "teaching literacy," not as a site of writing research or of specialized knowledge, despite the fact that the Moonlight Schools did offer innovative pedagogies and theories of literacy acquisition. This perception, I argue, stemmed from Stewart's consistent assertion that any literate person could teach the Moonlight Schools curriculum— that is, though the curriculum itself constituted specialized knowledge, the *use* of that curriculum did not require any special training: expertise was located in the textbook, in the theorist, *not* in the teacher herself. As argued above, Stewart's view reflected the "common sense" of elementary education of the early twentieth century; however, Stewart was the first public commentator to craft a thorough argument in favor of nonspecialized teachers. As such, we must credit (or blame) Stewart for helping to perpetuate a view of "teaching writing" as a form of service engaged in by a nonspecialized workforce.

As Rose, Crowley, and Colomb attest, despite the now-dominant "common sense" that all writing teachers must be trained, the belief that any literate person can teach writing continues to color perceptions of literacy educators at all levels but particularly within the university. That potential teachers, hired on a temporary basis at pay that, it could be said, is near enough to a volunteer's salary, are often required to demonstrate expertise in the field of literary studies—in the acts of reading, writing, and interpretation, rather than in the art of teaching or researching the processes of reading and writing—aptly illustrates the continuing power of the notion that "anyone can teach." In particular, the staffing practices employed for first-year composition and the lack of recognition of composition studies as a knowledge-making enterprise reflect the attitude Stewart articulated more than eighty years ago: knowledge is perceived as located in textbooks, in literary studies, or, at best, in advanced composition researchers; teachers require no specialized training to dispense this preexisting knowledge.

While it is beyond the scope of the current volume to suggest a solution to literacy studies' or composition studies' difficulty in gaining respect and recognition as academic disciplines, I do suggest that a more complete understanding of the history of public attitudes toward the teaching of writing can help literacy educators craft more effective responses to problematic public attitudes toward our work. And in analyzing the failures of the Moonlight Schools movement to establish itself as a knowledge-making enterprise, we have a cautionary tale that can guide our own efforts to publicize and gain academic recognition for our work. In particular, we can learn from Stewart's perpetuation of the very attitudes that undermined her status as an expert, as a maker of knowledge. We, too, must examine how we perpetuate problematic attitudes toward the teaching of writing, particularly in our own overlooking of the contributions to knowledge made by adjunct and graduate student faculty (see, for instance, Arnold et al.; Bousquet, Scott, and Parascondola; Theis). By failing to look to these teachers as sources of literacy theory and research, by failing to include them within our disciplinary discourse except as a "problem" that must be "solved" (see Crowley), we further reify the notion that teaching writing requires and generates no special expertise, and, in doing so, we further undermine our position within the academy. After all, if our primary purpose is viewed as "teaching writing," of what value are we as literacy educators if our work can be done by any literate person?

The Moonlight Schools, as well as the Americanizers, represent a sea change in public and institutional perceptions of what it meant to teach and study literacy. If we are to understand how our educational institutions have changed and failed to change, we must incorporate the narrative of the Moonlight Schools into our disciplinary history. If we are to improve our position within the academy and the general public, we must understand the history of attitudes toward the teaching of literacy. Though many organizations and individuals have influenced those attitudes, the Moonlight Schools must hold a prominent place as having generated discourses that continue to frame our work today.

An understanding of the Moonlight Schools and Americanization offers many benefits to literacy educators. By reading these narratives against our own historical narratives, we can gain perspective on how the stories we tell ourselves about our work promote particular ideologies, and we can thus make more informed decisions about how we represent our past and our present. By incorporating the Moonlight Schools and Americanization into our disciplinary knowledge, we can better understand our place in a continuum of literacy research. By understanding the roles that both Moonlight Schools advocates and Americanizers have played in creating a public discourse of teacher professionalization, we can better craft responses to public perceptions of our work as literacy educators.

Notes

References

Index

NOTES

1. Introduction

1. A literacy test was finally passed over presidential veto in 1917.

2. I use the term "native-born whites" to reflect racial divisions as they were imagined in the period of my historical survey. At that time, native-born whites were imagined as Anglo-Saxons of western European descent. While Protestantism was closely linked with the concept of native whiteness, Catholics of western European descent were by this time period typically also included within this concept, although religion and culture had in earlier decades led to differentiation between "Irish" and "white" (see Ignatiev).

2. Literacy, Crisis, and Educational Responses

1. Baldwin explains, "Education lost ground during [Edwin P. Morrow's] administration, as its share of the budget declined from 44.7 percent in 1910 to 38 percent in 1920. It fell to 30 percent by 1927" (119).

2. The Immigration Act of 1917 fined transportation companies for bringing illiterates into the country and required those companies to return excludable immigrants to their point of origin.

3. Developing Pedagogies for Illiterate Adults

1. See Baldwin regarding the Moonlight Schools' pedagogy; on Americanization pedagogies, see Dayton-Wood; McClymer, "Americanization Movement."

2. Script lessons are lines printed in cursive letters. Students were expected to copy these lines into their tablets (provided along with the readers).

3. Travel from isolated homesteads to school buildings could be treacherous in daylight due to the poor (or absent) roads that connected mountain settlements; traveling in the dark was nearly impossible. Schools were held on moonlit nights to help ensure student safety, and classes were kept to specific

time frames so that families would know exactly when to expect their Moonlight Schools students to return home.

4. In her notes for another textbook—one that does not appear to have been distributed—Stewart offers this list of values as ideal for students to learn: "cleanliness, good work, good words, good thoughts, banish fear, be cheerful, begin again, faith in the new, unselfishness, and Godliness" ("Report on Prison"). Drawing from this list, I am defining "middle-class values" as a set of behaviors and beliefs that emphasize the importance of cleanliness, hard work in "respectable" professions, church attendance, positive attitude, loyalty to one's community, and openness to education. Stewart omitted those values associated with poorer members of her local community, including loyalty to family, holding to traditional ways of behaving and believing, and independence.

5. Mountain people commonly collected wild-growing herbs, mushrooms, and berries.

6. Bibles were given as a reward to the first session's graduates. This practice was continued in later sessions when funds allowed.

7. R. E. Jaggers was my great-grandfather. He later became a professor of education at Eastern Kentucky University. It is perhaps worth mentioning, in light of Stewart's emphasis on volunteer teaching, that Jaggers later became a leading advocate for preservice training of teachers. It is also worth noting that he was, by his own account, totally illiterate until age seventeen.

8. Some studies of eye movement during reading had been conducted, but these studies did little to document comprehension or even the material being read.

9. The remaining time was devoted to introductory singing, math, and elective drills. While some drills featured reading and writing components, many were conducted orally.

10. For instance, phonemic lessons based on "standard" American speech (or the middle-class speech of Moonlight Schools teachers, many of whom were not locals) would not have accounted for the Appalachian rendering of some "i" inflections: "hire," for instance, rhymes with "car." Stewart *did* attempt to alter students' dialect through English drills, but such activity would have "hamper[ed]" initial reading efforts and potentially added to students' feelings of shame when encountering the written page.

11. In this publication and in her public speeches, Stewart forwarded two rationales for providing literacy to soldiers. She argued, on one hand, that illiterate soldiers were an impediment to the army, because they could not read orders, instruction manuals, or road signs. On the other hand, Stewart argued that sending illiterate men to the front amounted to a form of cruelty, because the men were, in essence, totally isolated from their families at home because they could not exchange letters with their loved ones.

12. Because I aim to analyze how Stewart drew on existing scholarship (and because Stewart's pedagogical approach changed very little from its original [1911] incarnation), my references to "Deweyan pedagogy" refer specifically to those texts that Dewey published before 1911, particularly *My Pedagogic Creed* (1897), *The School and Society* (1899), and *The Child and the Curriculum* (1902). Dewey had not yet fully theorized those elements of his pedagogy for which he is most remembered by modern scholars; in particular, his exploration of experiential pedagogies was not fully articulated until the publication of *Experience and Education* (1938). Similarly, Dewey does not explore the role of language in either psychology or education in his early texts; his primary theorization of language occurs in *Democracy and Education* (1916).

13. Because Stewart encouraged all her teaching corps to subscribe to educational journals, it is reasonable to believe that Stewart herself, through her access to these journals, would have been aware of, if not fully informed about, Dewey's work in elementary education.

14. Stewart did not have the resources—in terms of time or finances—to compose a new reader every year to address innovations in agriculture or other fields of interest to rural students. To ensure that new scientific and historical developments were communicated to students, the Kentucky Illiteracy Commission, under Stewart's leadership, published yearly bulletins with updated instructions for teachers and new lesson plans for elective drills. While many drill subjects remained constant from year to year, the material within the drills, especially drills on agriculture and horticulture, were altered to reflect new developments in both scientific research and state policies. Stewart also added drills that reflected current events. In 1918, following the US entry into World War I, the annual bulletin added drills on "The Nations in the War," "The Great World War," "America in the War," food use during the war, patriotism and patriotic quotations, the Red Cross, facts about the army, and the history and proper treatment of the American flag. The postwar 1919 bulletin replaces "America in the War" with a drill on "How America Helped Save the World" and omits the Red Cross drill in favor of a League of Nations lesson.

15. Stewart appears to have drawn these lessons from observations made during her 1920 trip to several reservations in the Dakotas. Her letters suggest that she thoroughly enjoyed the visit, which likely predisposed her to embrace Native American experiences in the textbook.

16. *Mother's First Book* is the only textbook that sought to appeal to Americanizers because Stewart composed her other broad-audience textbooks, the *Country Life Readers*, prior to, or immediately after, the United States entered World War I. As explained in chapter 4, though the Americanizers were already funded at higher levels than the Moonlight Schools, Americanization funding saw massive increases in response to the patriotic fervor the war created.

17. Though Stewart often sought to illustrate that rural women did not fit these stereotypes in her speeches, she nevertheless believed that many rural women *could* benefit from such lessons. But by publishing a text that responds to these characterizations by trying to "correct" uncouth behaviors, Stewart ultimately participates in reifying the stereotypes immigrant and rural women faced.

18. Americanizers did, of course, teach many lessons on "American life," which, in theory, taught students how to participate in society. However, extant data suggest that more often than not, these lessons consisted of platitudes rather than concrete explanations (see McClymer, "Americanization").

4. The Politics of Americanization

1. During World War I, Aronovici was the most vocal opponent of militant Americanization programs, yet here she acknowledges that illiteracy among the immigrants presents a major hurdle toward English-language acquisition.

2. Although rural schools suffered disproportionately from the effects of locally based funding, rural school boards were often among the most vocal opposition to increased state or federal control over education. If schools were placed under government auspices, the school board trustees believed they would be replaced by specially trained and/or more educated officials (and, in fact, they were).

3. And, as I have argued elsewhere, the 1910 census underrepresents illiteracy.

4. The Appalachian Regional Commission currently designates fifty-four counties as Appalachian, but one, McCreary, had not yet been formed in 1910.

5. By contrast, only six of the sixty-six non-Appalachian counties reported rates higher than 15 percent.

6. Stewart was not the only Kentuckian making such claims; David E. Whisnant explains that in 1913, Josiah Combs, a renowned scholar of Kentucky folk music, "lamented that more money was being spent to educate the 'thousands of foreigners that pour into our country monthly by way of New York harbor' than the 'virile and sturdy' Anglo-Saxon stock of the mountains" (92). As detailed in my introduction, William Goodell Frost, president of Berea College, is often cited as the first rhetorician to posit Appalachians' Anglo-Saxon identity as a counterpoint to immigrant cultures.

7. Americanizers' obsession with immigrants' food intake stemmed from two causes. First, many immigrants (and many natives) did not practice healthy eating habits, and settlement workers zeroed in on diet as a concrete way to improve the lives of immigrant children. More subtly, immigrants' eating practices were an identifiably different from natives' diets. Unlike race, personality traits, or education, all of which were ultimately rhetorically constructed, the presence of cabbage in one's home was an unmistakable, tangible, physical marker of "otherness" that could then be tangibly removed.

8. Unfortunately for Stewart, *Mother's First Book* was not published until the Americanization movement had begun to wane.

9. Neither the book nor Stewart's papers make clear whether the Mexican and Jewish mothers pictured were immigrants or natives; however, coupled with Stewart's reference to "racial groups," it is likely that contemporary readers would have thought of these women as immigrants.

10. In 1917, Stewart also refused education commissioner P. P. Claxton's offer to appoint her as specialist in adult education to the Bureau of Education. Though Stewart cited her work in Kentucky as the reason for her decision to decline, the position was also one that would have placed Stewart firmly in the field of immigrant education (Baldwin 107).

11. This trip was cancelled because many Americanization supporters voiced concerns that the National Illiteracy Crusade was "red."

12. In fact, Stewart's request that the census bureau release names of illiterates to Moonlight Schools organizers opened a key avenue of statistical evidence for all illiteracy workers, including Americanizers.

13. She excused the delay by saying that she had been in Europe and the Pacific Northwest and that her mail had not been efficiently forwarded; however, records of her correspondence demonstrate that she responded to more welcome mail with relative promptness during this period.

14. The department's name change reflected solely the absorption of the Illiteracy Committee.

5. Professionalizing Adult Education

1. Two speakers' employments were not identified. Though these speakers may have been elementary school teachers, a lack of designation in the *Addresses* may imply that the speaker is not currently employed or is changing jobs.

2. Other speakers include editors of educational publications, state inspectors, members of educational committees, and a medical doctor.

3. In fact, Baker is more inclusive than most NEA commentators—she includes a brief quote from a "spirited little third-grade teacher" in her argument for improved English teaching (432).

4. Though modern readers may interpret this statement as coercive—Stewart was, after all, the teachers' supervisor; could they have said no?—the request may also be interpreted as benign. In general during the early twentieth century, and particularly in small rural communities, social structures were predicated on reciprocal volunteerism; the teachers could have reasonably expected to be repaid in kind by community members.

5. Names of students have been altered in recognition of the fact that Stewart used students' work without permission.

6. Not surprising, immigrants' preferences seem to have been given no more than cursory consideration when teachers were assigned to courses; none of the major surveyors of Americanization programs reference any practice of consulting immigrants on their preferences for teachers (or, for that matter, pedagogy).

7. Though I have cited Mahoney, the first page of Mahoney's text is lifted—without attribution—from Thompson's *Schooling of the Immigrant*.

8. For reasons explained later in the text, she never received this funding.

9. The other responses rated above "discouragement" were "overtime work" and "illness or family circumstances."

10. Stewart's *Country Life Readers, First Book*, which advocates a course less than half as long as NACI's beginner course of the manual, contains four practice letters and a fifth letter from Stewart to students that could be used as a source of additional practice. Students were not considered to have passed the course until they wrote a letter to Stewart.

11. Even today, students who live in isolated hollers are not expected to attend schools during inclement weather; when schools issue "late-start" orders (colloquially termed Plan A or Plan B), opening schools at 9 or 10 A.M., these students are traditionally granted excused absences from their classwork.

6. Implications and Conclusions

1. For instance, James McKeen Cattell was a leading voice among eugenics advocates and was a key figure in "normaliz[ing] the performance of English-dominant, European American males from middle to upper class environments as the standard group by which reading performance is measured" (Willis 38). Robert Sessions Woodworth suggested that immigrants should be judged not on their national origin but rather on the basis of intelligence tests; he also argued that the results of the army tests of 1917 (which he helped to construct) demonstrated that "we have recently been receiving a rather unfavorable selection of immigrants in point of intelligence" (Berger et al. 74).

2. That is, standardized reading test of *basic* reading skills; colleges, including Harvard with its famous entrance examination, had been claiming to be assessing advanced reading and writing skills through tests and scales for many years.

3. Again, the various college entrance examinations in use at this time, as well as a variety of tests for secondary students, *assessed* the literacy skills of adults; however, these tests made no attempt to measure or study learning styles or processes of acquiring literacy. No controlled (or, indeed, uncontrolled) study had been conducted to established the benefits of particular teaching methods for teaching literacy.

4. Most universities that employ graduate students to teach composition courses provide some variety of training for these teachers; however, this training is most often conducted immediately before graduate students begin their first teaching assignment (i.e., the graduate students are assigned to teach *before* they have been instructed in teaching, so training is not a criteria by which teaching assignments are granted).

REFERENCES

Alderman, Lewis. "Adult Education and Citizenship." *National Education Association of the United States: Proceedings of the Sixty-Sixth Annual Meeting.* Washington: NEA, 1928. 131–33. Print.

———. "Emergency Relief and Adult Education." *School and Society* 38 (Dec. 1933): 717–19. Print.

Alderman, Lewis, et al. "Report of the Commission on Coordination in Adult Education." *National Education Association of the United States: Proceedings of the Sixty-Fifth Annual Meeting.* Washington: NEA, 1927. 327–32. Print.

American Association for Adult Education. *Annual Report of the Director 1934–1935.* New York: Amer. Assn. for Adult Educ., 1935.

Angelo, Richard. "A Brief Photo Essay on the History of Education in Kentucky." *University of Kentucky College of Education.* University of Kentucky, 18 Nov. 2008. Web. 13 Aug. 2010. <http://www.uky.edu/Education/EPE/Angelo/photohis01.html/>.

Appalachian Regional Commission. "Counties in Appalachia." *Appalachian Regional Commission.* Appalachian Regional Commission, n.d. Web. 12 Aug. 2010.

Arnold, Lisa, Laura Brady, Maggie Christensen, Joanne Baird Giordano, Holly Hassel, Ed Naglehout, Nathalie Singh-Corcoran, and Julie Staggers. "Forum on the Profession." *College English* 73.4 (2011): 409–27. Print.

Aronovici, Carol. "Americanization: Its Meaning and Function." *American Journal of Sociology* 25.6 (1920): 695–730. Print.

Baker, Adelaide Steele. "English in the Elementary Schools." *Journal of Proceedings and Addresses of the National Education Association of the United States.* Ann Arbor: NEA, 1910. 430–34. Print.

Baldwin, Yvonne Honeycutt. *Cora Wilson Stewart and Kentucky's Moonlight Schools: Fighting for Literacy in America.* Lexington: U of Kentucky P, 2006. Print.

Balmuth, Miriam. *Roots of Phonics: A Historical Introduction.* New York: McGraw-Hill, 1982. Print.

Barrett, James R. "Americanization from the Bottom Up: Immigration and the Remaking of the Working Class in the United States, 1880–1930." *Journal of American History* 79.3 (1992): 996–1020. Print.

Batteau, Allen. *The Invention of Appalachia*. Tucson: U of Arizona P, 1990. Print.

Berger, Allen, Dixie D. Massey, Kristin Stoll, and Aviva Gray. "Robert Sessions Woodworth (1869–1962): Dean of Psychologists." Israel and Monaghan 61–79.

Berlin, James. *Rhetoric and Reality: Writing Instruction in American Colleges, 1900–1985*. Carbondale: Southern Illinois UP, 1987. Print.

Billings, Dwight, Gurney Norman, and Katherine Ledford, eds. *Back Talk from Appalachia: Confronting Stereotypes*. Lexington: U of Kentucky P, 1999. Print.

Bledstein, Burton. *The Culture of Professionalism: The Middle Class and the Development of Higher Education in America*. New York: Norton, 1976. Print.

Bogardus, Emory Stephen. *Essentials of Americanization*. Rev. ed. Los Angeles: U of Southern California P, 1920. Print.

Boswell, Helen Varick. "Promoting Americanization." *Annals of the American Academy of Political and Social Science* 64 (Mar. 1916): 204–9. Print.

Bousquet, Marc, Tony Scott, and Leo Parascondola, eds. *Tenured Bosses and Disposable Teachers: Writing Instruction in the Managed University*. Carbondale: Southern Illinois UP, 2004. Print.

Brandt, Deborah. "Drafting U.S. Literacy." *College English* 66.5 (2004): 485–502. Print.

———. *Literacy in American Lives*. New York: Cambridge UP, 2001. Print.

Bush, George W. Foreword. *Proposal: No Child Left Behind; President Bush's Education Reform Act*. Rethinking Schools. 2001. Web. 30 Apr. 2014. <http://www.rethinkingschools.org/static/special_reports/bushplan/no-child-left-behind.pdf>.

Butler, Fred. Preface. *Training Teachers for Americanization: A Course of Study for Normal Schools and Teachers' Institutes*. Bulletin no. 20. Ed. John Mahoney. Washington: GPO, 1919. Print.

Button, H. Warren, and Eugene F. Provenzo Jr. *History of Education and Culture in America*. New York: Prentice-Hall, 1983. Print.

Butts, R. Freeman, and Lawrence Cremin. *A History of Education in American Culture*. New York: Holt, 1953. Print.

California Commission of Immigration and Housing. *The Annual Report of the Commission of Immigration and Housing of California*. Sacramento: California State Printing Office, 1919.

Carlson, Robert A. *The Quest for Conformity: Americanization through Education*. New York: Wiley, 1975. Print.

Claxton, P. P. "Letter of Transmittal." Mahoney 5.

Cody, Frank. "Americanization Courses in the Public Schools." *English Journal* 7.10 (1918): 615–22. Print.

Coffman, L. D. "Training for National Service in Normal Schools." *Journal of the National Education Association* 3.1 (1918): 167–69. Print.

Colomb, Gregory. "Franchising the Future." *College Composition and Communication* 62.1 (2010): 11–30. Print.

Cong. Rec. 14 Feb. 1914: 4188–92. Print.

Cook, Wanda. *Adult Literacy Education in the United States*. Newark: Intl. Reading Assoc., 1977. Print.

Cornelius, Janet. "Slave Testimony: 'We Slipped and Learned to Read.'" *When I Can Read My Title Clear: Literacy, Slavery, and Religion in the Antebellum South*. Columbia: U of South Carolina P, 1992. 59–84. Print.

Cremin, Lawrence. *The Transformation of the School: Progressivism in American Education, 1876–1957*. New York: Knopf, 1961. Print.

Crowley, Sharon. *Composition in the University: Historical and Polemical Essays*. Pittsburgh: U of Pittsburgh P, 1998. Print.

Cubberley, Ellwood. *Changing Conceptions of Education*. Boston: Houghton Mifflin, 1909. Print.

Dauben, Joseph Warren, and Christoph Scriba, eds. *Writing the History of Mathematics: Its Historical Development*. Basel: Birkhauser, 2002. Print.

Dayton-Wood, Amy. "Teaching English for 'A Better America.'" *Rhetoric Review* 27.4 (2008): 397–414. Print.

De Garmo, Mrs. Frank. "The Humanity of Highways." *Journal of Proceedings and Addresses of the National Education Association of the United States*. Ann Arbor: NEA, 1912. 301–7. Print.

Deming, Robert. "The Department of Adult Education, Its Status and Future." *National Education Association of the United States: Proceedings of the Sixty-Fifth Annual Meeting*. Washington: NEA, 1927. 295–99. Print.

———."Federal Aspects of and Responsibilities in the Reduction of Illiteracy and Training for Citizenship." *National Education Association of the United States: Proceedings of the Sixty-Seventh Annual Meeting*. Washington: NEA, 1929. 284–86. Print.

———. "How Are We 'Training' Adult Immigrants for Intelligent Citizenship?" *National Education Association of the United States: Proceedings of the Sixty-Seventh Annual Meeting*. Washington: NEA, 1929. 313. Print.

Department of Superintendence. "Resolutions of the Department of Superintendence, Chicago, February 24–March 1." *Addresses and Proceedings of the Fifty-Seventh Annual Meeting Held at Milwaukee, Wisconsin June 28–July 5, 1919*. Washington: NEA, 1919. Print.

Dewey, John. *The Child and the Curriculum*. Chicago: U of Chicago P, 1902. Print.

———. *My Pedagogic Creed*. New York: Kellogg, 1898. Print.

Dodge, Allen. "Report of the Committee on Education of the House of Representatives." *American Educational Thought: Essays from 1640–1940*. Ed. Andrew J. Milson. Charlotte: Information Age, 2010. Print.

Driver, Lee. "The Organization of Public Education for Service in the New Democracy." *Addresses and Proceedings of the Fifty-Seventh Annual Meeting Held at Milwaukee, Wisconsin June 28–July 5, 1919.* Washington: NEA, 1919. Print.

"Educational Div. No. 1, Sch. Dist. No. 6." School census notes, box 64. Stewart Papers.

"Educational Div. No. 2, Sch. Dist. No. 9." School census notes, box 64. Stewart Papers.

Eller, Ronald. Foreword. Billings, Norman, and Ledford ix–xi.

———. "Harry Caudill and the Burden of Mountain Liberalism." *Critical Essays in Appalachian Life and Culture: Proceedings of the Fifth Annual Appalachian Studies Conference.* Ed. Rick Simon. Boone: Appalachian Consortium, 1982. Print.

Ellsworth, Clayton S. "The Coming of Rural Consolidated Schools to the Ohio Valley, 1892–1912." *Agricultural History* 30.3 (1956): 119–28. Print.

Estes, Florence S. "Cora Wilson Stewart and the Moonlight Schools of Kentucky, 1911–1920: A Case Study in the Rhetorical Uses of Literacy." PhD diss. University of Kentucky, 1988. Print.

Fisher, Steve. "As the World Turns: The Melodrama of Harry Caudill." *Appalachian Journal* 2.3 (1984): 268–73. Print.

Flesch, Rudolph. *Why Johnny Can't Read: And What You Can Do about It.* New York: Harper, 1955. Print.

Freidson, Eliot. *Professionalism Reborn: Theory, Prophecy, and Policy.* Chicago: U of Chicago P, 1994. Print.

Frost, William Goodell. "Our Contemporary Ancestors in the Southern Mountains." *Atlantic Monthly* 83 (1899): 311–19. Rpt. in New York: Atlantic Monthly, 1899. *Google Books.* Web. 7 Nov. 2010.

Gee, James. *Social Linguistics and Literacies: Ideologies and Discourses.* New York: Taylor and Francis, 2008. Print.

Gere, Anne Ruggles. *Intimate Practices: Literacy and Cultural Work in U.S. Women's Clubs, 1880–1920.* Urbana: U of Illinois P, 1997. Print.

Goldin, Claudia, and Gary Libecap. *The Regulated Economy: A Historical Approach to Political Economy.* Chicago: U of Chicago P, 1994. Print.

Gordon, Edward, and Elaine Gordon. *Literacy in America: Historic Journey and Current Solutions.* Westport: Praeger, 2003. Print.

Graff, Harvey. *The Literacy Myth: Cultural Integration and Social Structure in the Nineteenth Century.* New Brunswick: Transaction, 1991. Print.

Grattan, Clinton Hartley. *In Quest of Knowledge: A Historical Perspective on Adult Education.* Manchester: Ayer, 1978. Print.

Gray, Robert Floyd. "The Training of Americanization Teachers." *Educational Review* 61 (1921): 224–29. Print.

Gray, William S. *Manual for Teachers of Adult Illiterates.* Washington: Natl. Advisory Committee on Illiteracy, 1930. Print.

Gray, William S., Bernice Elizabeth Leary, and Joint Committee on the Reading Interests and Habits of Adults. *What Makes a Book Readable: With Special Reference to Adults of Limited Reading Ability*. Chicago: U of Chicago P, 1935. Print.

Greenwood, James. "Strengthening the Work in the Elementary Grades." *Journal of Proceedings and Addresses of the National Education Association of the United States*. Ann Arbor: NEA, 1910. 436–40. Print.

Hall, Prescott. "The Recent History of Immigration and Immigration Restriction." *Journal of Political Economy* 21.8 (1913): 735–51. Print.

Hayes, D. W. "What the Normal Schools Can Do and Ought to Do with the Training of Teachers for Rural Communities." *Journal of Proceedings and Addresses of the National Education Association of the United States*. Ann Arbor: NEA, 1912. 546–52. Print.

Hennen, John. *The Americanization of West Virginia: Creating a Modern Industrial State*. Lexington: U of Kentucky P, 1996. Print.

Hennessy, Miss. "Organization in St. Louis." *Proceedings of the Second Biennial Convention of the National Women's Trade Union League of America*. National Women's Trade Union League, 1909. 46. Print.

Herbst, Jurgen. *And Sadly Teach: Teacher Education and Professionalization in American Culture*. Madison: U of Wisconsin P, 1989. Print.

"Hidden America: Children of the Mountains, A." *20/20*. ABC. WDKY, Lexington. 13 Feb. 2007. Television.

Higham, John. 1955. *Strangers in the Land: Patterns of American Nativism, 1860–1925*. New York: Atheneum, 1975. Print.

Hill, Howard. "The Americanization Movement." *American Journal of Sociology* 24.6 (1919): 609–42. Print.

Horner, Bruce, and John Trimbur. "English Only and U.S. College Composition." *College Composition and Communication* 53.4 (2002): 594–630. Print.

Horsman, Reginald. *Race and Manifest Destiny: The Origins of American Racial Anglo-Saxonism*. Cambridge: Harvard UP, 1981. Print.

Huebner, Grover. "The Americanization of the Immigrant." *Annals of the American Academy of Political and Social Science* 27 (May 1906): 191–213. Print.

Ignatiev, Noel. *How the Irish Became White*. New York: Routledge, 1995. Print.

International Reading Association, Jill Fitzgerald, and H. Alan Robinson, eds. *Reading Comprehension Instruction, 1783–1987: A Review of Research and Trends*. Newark: Intl. Reading Assoc., 1990. Print.

Israel, Susan, and E. Jennifer Monaghan, eds. *Shaping the Reading Field: The Impact of Early Reading Pioneers, Scientific Research, and Progressive Ideas*. Newark: Intl. Reading Assoc., 2007. Print.

Kellor, Frances. "Industrial Americanization." *American Industries* 19 (1919): 35. Print.

Kendall, Constance. *The Worlds We Deliver: Confronting the Consequences of Believing in Literacy*. PhD diss. University of Miami (Ohio), 2005. Print.

Kentucky Illiteracy Commission. "Facts Concerning Moonlight School Work." Pamphlet. 1919. Cora Wilson Stewart Collection, Camden-Carroll Library, Morehead State University, Morehead, Kentucky.

Keppel, Mark. "Rural-School Organization and Administration." *Journal of Proceedings and Addresses of the National Education Association of the United States*. Ann Arbor: NEA, 1913. 718–19. Print.

Kett, Joseph F. *The Pursuit of Knowledge under Difficulties: From Self-Improvement to Adult Education in American 1750–1990*. Stanford: Stanford UP, 1994. Print.

Knowles, Malcolm Shepard. *A History of the Adult Education Movement in the United States*. Malabar: Krieger, 1994. Print.

Korman, Gerd. *Industrialization, Immigrants, and Americanizers: The View from Milwaukee, 1866–1921*. Madison: State Hist. Soc. of Wisconsin, 1967. Print.

Kramer, Lloyd, Donald Reid, and William L. Barney, eds. *Learning History in America: Schools, Cultures, and Politics*. Minneapolis: U of Minnesota P, 1994. Print.

Larson, Magali Sarfatti. *The Rise of Professionalism: A Sociological Analysis*. Berkeley: U of California P, 1977. Print.

Lowe, Gary R., and P. Nelson Reid, eds. *The Professionalization of Poverty: Social Work and the Poor in the Twentieth Century*. New York: de Gruyter, 1999. Print.

Luke, Robert A. *The NEA and Adult Education: A Historical Review: 1921–1972*. Self-published, 1992. Print.

MacCormack, D. W. Letter to Cora Wilson Stewart. 23 Sept. 1933. Box 29. Stewart Papers.

Mahoney, John J. *Training Teachers for Americanization: A Course of Study for Normal Schools and Teachers' Institutes*. Bulletin no. 20. Washington: GPO, 1920. Print.

Maloney, John. *The Professionalization of Economics: Alfred Marshall and the Dominance of Orthodoxy*. New Brunswick: Transaction, 1991. Print.

Mann, Horace. "A Lecture on the Best Mode of Preparing and Using Spelling Books: Delivered before the American Institute of Instruction, August, 1841." Part 2. *Common School Journal* 4.2 (1842): 25–32. Print.

———. "A Lecture on the Best Mode of Preparing and Using Spelling Books: Delivered before the American Institute of Instruction, August, 1841." Part 3. *Common School Journal* 4.3 (1842): 40–48. Print.

McBride, Paul. "Peter Roberts and the YMCA Americanization Program, 1907–World War I." *Pennsylvania History* 44.2 (1977): 145–62. Print.

McClymer, John F. "The Americanization Movement and the Education of the Foreign-Born Adult, 1914–25." Weiss, *American Education* 96–116.

———. "Gender and the 'American Way of Life': Women and the Americanization Movement." *Journal of American Ethnic History* 10.3 (1991): 3–20. Print.

Miller, Herbert Adolphus. *The School and the Immigrant*. Cleveland: Survey Committee of the Cleveland Foundation, 1916. Print.

Moore, Margaret. *Citizenship Training of Adult Immigrants in the United States: Its Status in Relation to the Census of 1920*. Washington: GPO, 1925. Print.

Mortensen, Peter. "Literacy and Regional Difference: Problems with the Invention of Appalachia." 43rd Conference on College Composition and Communication. Cincinnati, Ohio. 19–21 Mar. 1992\). ERIC no. 346 248. Print.

Moskovitz, Cary, and Michael Petit. "Insiders and Outsiders: Redrawing the Boundaries of the Writing Program." *WPA Journal* 31.1–2 (2007): 86–103. Print.

"National Advisory Committee on Illiteracy." *Elementary School Journal* 30.5 (1930): 321–22. Print.

Nelms, Willie. *Cora Wilson Stewart: Crusader Against Illiteracy*. Jefferson: McFarland, 1997. Print.

Nestos, R. A. Letter to Cora Wilson Stewart. 22 Feb. 1930. Box 13. Stewart Papers.

———. Letter to Cora Wilson Stewart. 15 Sept. 1930. Box 13. Stewart Papers.

Nevins, Allan. *Ford: The Times, the Man, the Company*. New York: Scribner's, 1954. Print.

New York League. "New York Women's League Reports." *Proceedings of the Second Biennial Convention of the National Women's Trade Union League of America*. Natl. Women's Trade Union League, 1909. 16–17. Print.

O'Brien, Kenneth B., Jr. "Americanization and the Supreme Court: The 1920's." *American Quarterly* 13.2 (1961): 161–71. Print.

Olneck, Michael R. "Americanization and the Education of Immigrants, 1900–1925: An Analysis of Symbolic Action." *American Journal of Education* 97.4 (1989): 398–423. Print.

Partridge, Sandra K. "France Kellor and the American Arbitration Association." *Dispute Resolution Journal* (Feb.–Apr. 2012): 17–21. Print.

Pavlenko, Aneta. "'We Have Room for But One Language Here': Language and National Identity in the US at the Turn of the 20th Century." *Multilingua* 21 (2002): 163–96. Print.

Pollard, Rebecca. *A Complete Manual: Pollard's Synthetic Method of Reading and Spelling*. New York: Amer. Book, 1889. Print.

Powell, Michael. *From Patrician to Professional Elite: The Transformation of the New York City Bar Association*. New York: Sage Foundation, 1988. Print.

Reed, Frank. "Half-Educated Generation." *Washington Post* 29 Dec. 1979: A11. Print.

Roberts, Peter. *The Problem of Americanization*. New York: Macmillan, 1920. Print.

Rodgers, Geraldine. *The History of Beginning Reading Instruction: From Teaching by Sound to Teaching by Meaning*. 3 vols. Bloomington: Authorhouse, 2001. Print.

Roediger, David R. *Working toward Whiteness: How America's Immigrants Became White*. New York: Basic, 2005. Print.

Roosevelt, Theodore. "Letter from Theodore Roosevelt to the Progressive National Committee." *The Progressive Party: Its Record from January to July, 1916, Including Statements and Speeches of Theodore Roosevelt.* Ed. Executive Committee of the Progressive National Committee. New York: Press of the Mail, 1916. Print.

Rose, Mike. "Narrowing the Mind and Page: Writers and Cognitive Reductionism." *Cross Talk in Comp Theory: A Reader.* Ed. Victor Villanueva. Urbana: NCTE, 2003. 345–85. Print.

Royster, Jacquelyn Jones. *Traces of a Stream: Literacy and Social Change Among African American Women.* Pittsburgh: U of Pittsburgh P, 2000. Print.

Salomone, Rosemary C. *True American: Language, Identity, and the Education of Immigrant Children.* Cambridge: Harvard UP, 2010. Print.

School Journal. Clipping. 18 May 1916. Untitled scrapbook of news clippings. Stewart Papers.

Scott, Fred Newton. "English Composition as a Mode of Behavior." *English Journal* 11.8 (1922): 463–73. Print.

Sears, Lou Ann. "Edward Lee Thorndike (1874–1949): A Look at His Contributions to Learning and Reading." Israel and Monaghan 119–39.

Shapiro, Henry D. *Appalachia on Our Mind: The Southern Mountains and Mountaineers in the American Consciousness, 1870–1920.* Chapel Hill: U of North Carolina P, 1978. Print.

Sharer, Wendy. *Vote and Voice: Women's Organizations and Political Literacy, 1915–1930.* Carbondale: Southern Illinois UP, 2004. Print.

Sharlip, William, and Albert Owens. *Adult Immigrant Education: Its Scope, Content, and Methods.* New York: Macmillan, 1925. Print.

Sheils, Merrill. "Why Johnny Can't Write." *Newsweek* 8 Dec. 1975: 58–65. Print.

Shor, Ira. *Culture Wars: School and Society in the Conservative Restoration, 1969–1984.* Chicago: U of Chicago P, 1992. Print.

———. *When Students Have Power: Negotiating Authority in Critical Pedagogy.* Chicago: U of Chicago P, 1996. Print.

Smith, Nila Banton. *American Reading Instruction: Its Development and Its Significance in Gaining Perspective on Current Practices in Reading.* Spec. ed. Newark: Intl. Reading Assoc., 2002. Print.

Smith, W. C. "Training Teachers for the Americanization Problem." *Proceedings Americanization Conference.* Washington: GPO, 1919. 108–14. Print.

Smith, W. C., Marguerite H. Burnett, Alonzo G. Grace, R. C. Deming, and A. W. Castle. Untitled position statement. 2 Jul. 1929. Box 13. Stewart Papers.

Soltow, Lee, and Edward Stevens. *The Rise of Literacy and the Common School in the United States: A Socioeconomic Analysis to 1870.* Chicago: U of Chicago P, 1981. Print.

Stewart, Cora Wilson. "A Call to the Teachers." 1917. Box 17, Misc. Material. Stewart Papers.

———. *Country Life Readers—First Book*. Atlanta: Johnson, 1915. Print.

———. *Country Life Readers—Second Book*. Richmond: Johnson, 1916. Print.

———. "Delivered before the General Federation of Women's Clubs, Chautauqua, New York, June 1922." Box 45, General Speeches. Stewart Papers.

———. "Illiteracy as a Factor in the Crime Situation." *National Education Association of the United States: Proceedings of the Seventieth Annual Meeting*. Washington: NEA, 1932. 52–57. Print.

———. *The Indian's First Book*. Box 30, Illiteracy and Indians. Stewart Papers.

———. Letter to A. E. Winship, 14 Dec. 1925. Box 11. Stewart Papers.

———. Letter to Dr. Finley, 8 Feb. 1930. Box 13. Stewart Papers.

———. Letter to Henry Allen, 17 Oct. 1929. Box 13. Stewart Papers.

———. Letter to Henry Allen, 3 Dec. 1930. Box 13. Stewart Papers.

———. Letter to Herbert Houston, 28 Oct. 1929. Box 13. Stewart Papers.

———. Letter to Herbert Houston, 23 May 1930. Box 13. Stewart Papers.

———. Letter to Lela Mae Stiles, 29 July 1922. Box 13. Stewart Papers.

———. Letter to R. A. Nestos, 9 Jan. 1930. Box 13. Stewart Papers.

———. Letter to R. A. Nestos, 31 May 1930. Box 13. Stewart Papers.

———. Letter to R. A. Nestos, 11 Sept. 1930. Box 13. Stewart Papers.

———. Letter to Robert Deming, 14 Dec. 1925. Box 11. Stewart Papers.

———. Letter to Robert Deming, 23 Jan. 1926. Box 12. Stewart Papers.

———. Letter to T. H. Harris, 26 Aug. 1930. Box 13. Stewart Papers.

———. "Moonlight Schools: Address Delivered Before Kansas State Teachers Association, November 1915." Box 45, General Speeches. Stewart Papers.

———. *Moonlight Schools Course of Study: Reconstruction Number*. Frankfort: Kentucky Illiteracy Commission, 1919. Print.

———. *Moonlight Schools Course of Study: War Number*. Frankfort: Kentucky Illiteracy Commission, 1918. Print.

———. *Moonlight Schools: For the Emancipation of Adult Illiterates*. New York: Dutton, 1922. Print.

———. *Mother's First Book*. Richmond: Johnson, 1930. Print.

———. Papers. 1900–40. University of Kentucky Special Collections, Margaret I. King Library, Lexington.

———. "Radio Address, December 10, 1933." Box 14. Stewart Papers.

———. "Report of Committee on Adult Illiteracy." *National Education Association of the United States: Addresses and Proceedings of the Sixtieth Annual Meeting*. Washington: NEA, 1922. 453–56. Print.

———. "Report of the Illiteracy Committee of the National Council of Education." *National Education Association of the United States: Proceedings of the Sixty-Sixth Annual Meeting*. Washington: NEA, 1928. 246–52. Print.

———. "Report on Prison Reader." Undated [ca. 1926]. Box 54, *Prison Reader*. Stewart Papers.

———. *The Soldier's First Book.* Association Press, 1918. Print.

———. Untitled speech. Box 45, General Speeches. Stewart Papers. Includes note "Part of Birmingham, Alabama Speech" in what appears to be Stewart's handwriting.

———. "War-Modified Education and Illiteracy." *Journal of the National Education Association* 3.1 (1918): 117–20. Print.

———. "World Conference on Education, San Francisco, Cal. July 1923." Box 45, General Speeches. Stewart Papers.

Talbot, Winthrop. "Illiteracy and Democracy." *North American Review* 202.721 (1915): 873–78. Print.

Theis, Jeffrey. "Collegiality and the Department Mailbox: Subdivide and Conquer." *Profession* (2006): 87–94. Print.

Thompson, Frank V. *Schooling of the Immigrant.* New York: Harper, 1920. Print.

Thorndike, Edward Lee. 1927. *The Measurement of Intelligence.* New York: Arno, 1973. Print.

Thorndike, Edward Lee, Elsie Oschrin Bregman, John Warren Tilton, and Ella Woodyard. *Adult Learning.* New York: Macmillan, 1928. Print.

Thorngate, Ella. "Americanization in Omaha." *English Journal* 9.3 (1920): 123–28. Print.

Trachsel, Mary. *Institutionalizing Literacy: The Historical Role of College Entrance Examinations in English.* Carbondale: Southern Illinois UP, 1992. Print.

Trimbur, John. "Literacy and the Discourse of Crisis." *The Politics of Writing Instruction: Postsecondary.* Ed. Richard Bullock, Trimbur, and Charles Schuster. Upper Montclair: Boynton/Cook, 1991. 277–95. Print.

20 USC Sec. 6301. No Child Left Behind Act. 2001. Print.

United States. Bureau of the Census. *Thirteenth Census of the United States, Taken in 1910: Abstract of the Census.* Washington: GPO, 1913. Print.

———. ———. *Thirteenth Census of the United States, Taken in 1910: Statistics for Kentucky.* Washington: GPO, 1913. Print.

———. Bureau of Education. "Illiteracy in the United States and an Experiment for Its Elimination." Bulletin 19.20. Washington: GPO, 1917. Print.

———. Bureau of Naturalization. *Teacher's Manual to Accompany Part 1—Federal Citizenship Textbook, English.* Washington: GPO, 1922. Print.

———. Cong. House. Committee on Education. *To Promote the Education of Native Illiterates.* Hearing. 14 Feb. 1919. 65th Cong., 3rd sess. Washington: GPO, 1919. Print. <http://books.google.com/books?id=e-CoDAkn2jAC&printsec=frontcover#v=onepage&q&f=false>. Rpt. of *Illiteracy in the United States and an Experiment for Its Elimination.* 35–66.

———. ———. ———. Committee on Immigration and Naturalization. *Education and Americanization.* Hearing. 16, 17, 23, 27 Oct. 1919. 66th Cong.,

1st sess. Washington: GPO, 1919. Print.

———. Dept. of Labor. *Annual Report of the Commissioner General of Immigration to the Secretary of Labor.* Washington: GPO, 1919. Print.

———. ———. *Annual Report of the Commissioner General of Immigration to the Secretary of Labor.* Washington: GPO, 1921. Print.

University of Kentucky College of Education. "KERA Information." *University of Kentucky College of Education,* 18 Feb. 2010. Web. 3 Dec. 2010.

Vought, Hans P. *The Bully Pulpit and the Melting Pot: American Presidents and the Immigrant, 1897–1933.* Macon: Mercer UP, 2004. Print.

Ward, Robert. "The Restriction of Immigration." *North American Review* 179.573 (1904): 226–37. Print.

Weiss, Bernard J., ed. *American Education and the European Immigrant: 1840–1940.* Urbana: U of Illinois P, 1982. Print.

———. Introduction. Weiss, *American Education* xi–xxviii.

Whelan, Jean. "American Nursing: A Blueprint to the Past." *Nursing History and Health Care.* University of Pennsylvania School of Nursing. 2014. Web. 28 Apr. 2014. <http://www.nursing.upenn.edu/nhhc/Pages/AmericanNursingIntroduction.aspx>.

Whisnant, David E. *All That Is Native and Fine: The Politics of Culture in an American Region.* 25th ann. ed. Chapel Hill: U of North Carolina P, 2009. Print.

White, Kate. "Inherent Contradictions: Rhetorical Education for Citizenship in the General Federation of Women's Clubs." Conference on College Composition and Communication. Atlanta, Georgia. 22 Mar. 2011. Lecture.

Williams, Bronwyn. "Seeking New Worlds." *College Composition and Communication* 62.1 (2010): 127–46. Print.

Willis, Arlette Ingram. "James McKeen Cattell (1860–1944): His Life and Contributions to Reading Research." Israel and Monaghan 35–60.

Wilson, Warren. "A Social and Educational Survey of the Rural Community." *Journal of Proceedings and Addresses of the National Education Association of the United States.* Ann Arbor: NEA, 1912. 281–86. Print.

Wilson, Woodrow. "Proper Tests of Immigrants (January 28, 1915): Veto Message of the Literacy Test Bill." *Selected Addresses and Public Papers of Woodrow Wilson.* Ed. Albert Bushnell Hart. New York: Boni and Liveright, 1918. 67–70. Print.

Winter, Mrs. Thomas G. "General Federation Club News." *American Club Woman Magazine* 13.1 (1917): 3–4. Print.

INDEX

SAMANTHA NECAMP teaches in the Postsecondary Literacy Instruction Certificate Program in the School of Education at the University of Cincinnati. Her work has appeared in such journals as *College Composition and Communication*, the *Journal of Appalachian Studies*, and the *Aldous Huxley Annual*.